T0062981

The Inception of Banaras Hindu University:
Who was the Founder
in the light of Historical Documents?

Tejakar Jha

PARTRIDGE
A Penguin Random House Company

ISBN: Hardcover   978-1-4828-5249-3
             Softcover   978-1-4828-5248-6
             eBook   978-1-4828-5247-9

Print information available on the last page.

To order additional copies of this book, contact
Partridge India
000 800 10062 62
orders.india@partridgepublishing.com

www.partridgepublishing.com/india

Preface

At the outset, I would like to state that I am not an academic by profession. However, I believe that it is an obligation of at least every educated citizen to have some sort of epistemic interest, that is, interest in knowing what happened before in the context of what obtains today. It is this belief that prevailed on me to search out the works of British painters and travellers (from 1780 to 1850) on Bihar, which were published in one volume in Kameshwar Singh Bihar Heritage Series in 2008. Further, I also engaged myself in preparing a pictorial biography of late Dr. Rajendra Prasad, the first President of India. This biography was published by Bihar State Archives in 2011. A few months before, in 2010, a volume containing a few records and documents (preserved in the archive of Maharajadhiraja Kameshwar Singh Kalyani Foundation) regarding the activities of Maharaja Rameshwara Singh (1860-1929) of Darbhanga was published. This volume includes some evidence of his contribution to the creation of Banaras Hindu University (B.H.U.). This aroused my curiosity to know more about him.

Subsequently, I had to visit the archive of the said Foundation (which has a rich collection of photographs of personages and events of colonial days) for collecting the photographs of Dr. Rajendra Prasad. At Darbhanga, I also got the opportunity of looking into the files of letters and other documents concerning Rameshwara Singh. I was astonished to find out quite a number of papers related to the movement for the Hindu University revealing what he (Rameshwara Singh) had done for the establishment of B.H.U. I was then prompted to collect relevant documents from British Libraries, London. Simultaneously, I also began to consult books/ theses written so far in this context. Gradually, sufficient material was procured and as I went through the papers, I was left in no doubt that the current and popular notion regarding the 'Founder' of B.H.U. is in fact a flawed and incorrect understanding of the history of its establishment (on 4 February, 1916). Let me state here that it has not been my intention to please one section of society and ruffle feathers of another. History is said to be a debate without end, which, perhaps, continues without even being visible. The issue of the establishment of B.H.U. (the first denominational university in the country), though supposed to be settled today, yet, appeared to be open to debate. And, so, I thought it desirable to make efforts for contributing to the debate in this context as far as possible on the basis of historical records/documents in order to facilitate the making of the history of the inception of B.H.U. more scientific and truthful.

As soon as some of the documents were collected, I thought it proper to bring them to the notice of some eminent historians. I contacted first Professor Ramachandra Guha, one of the most renowned historians/social scientists of the country, whose response was so encouraging and prompt that it gave me much confidence for pursuing my endeavour further. I shall always remain deeply indebted to him. I also sent copies of a few documents to Dr. John A. Rorabacher who perused them and then passed them on to Dr. Stephen Henningham. Both of them sent their messages appreciating my approach and efforts and also gave valuable suggestions. My debt to them is great. I used to consult Dr. Hetukar Jha (retd. Professor of Sociology, Patna University) while working on this project. His insightful comments made it possible for me to pursue this project rather smoothly. I am indebtd to him. Besides, my thanks are due to my friends Ashish Sinha, John Martin Thomas, Vaidurya Pratap Shahi who always extended their cooperation. Neeraj Labh was kind enough to go through the manuscript and helped me in reading and correcting the proofs. I am grateful to him. I am thankful to the authorities of Maharajadhiraja Kameshwar Singh Kalyani Foundation (Darbhanga, Bihar) and those of British Libraries, London, for granting me access to their archives. Shweta Sinha always remained behind me. She took up the burden of our professional obligations on her own shoulders and helped me thereby to devote all my time to my project. I shall always remain indebted to her.

Tejakar Jha

Chapter 1

Prelude

The course of modern higher education in India began to take shape since the arrival of colonial power. Initially, for a long time until about 1882, the power to create and organize educational institutions remained in the hands of state authorities. Then, the government[1] "...adopted a policy of <u>Lassez faire</u> in education ... It declared that its duty was to pioneer the way... This policy accelerated the growth of higher education," and paved the way for the rise of private enterprise. Besides, the Indian elites by the late nineteenth century, it seems, had become quite conscious of the difference between Indian culture and that of colonizer. They considered that[2] "in the spiritual domain the East was superior to West". Further, according to Partha Chatterjee, in the eyes of Indian elites[3], "what was necessary was to cultivate the material techniques of modern western civilization <u>while retaining and strengthening the distinctive spiritual essence of the national culture</u>."(emphasis added). Subsequently, it seems, this ideological stand came to dominate the ethos of the socio-cultural milieu of the country. This enthused some individuals who began thinking of establishing a university, based on Western model. And these institutions were supposed to have institutionalized arrangement for promoting the knowledge of Indian spiritualism and theology. Consequently, perhaps, this trend gave rise to the idea for creating a Hindu University in Banaras.

Of all those who might have been thinking of the need of such a university, three persons came forward to take lead in this context. There was Annie Besant, an eminent scholar of Indian spiritual tradition and a prominent Theosophist. She had played a key role in **establishing Central Hindu College** in Banaras in 1898[4], "put forward the idea of establishing a university at Banaras under the name of "The University of India". In 1907 she prepared a memorial for the grant of Royal Charter for the establishment of the University."

Another notable person was Madan Mohan Malaviya, a lawyer and journalist (in the United Provinces) who had joined Indian National Congress in 1886. It is said that he prepared a scheme for a Hindu University in 1904[5], "that was circulated in October 1905 and was then discussed in December 1905 ... lastly, it was laid before the Sanatan Dharma Mahasabha... held at Allahabad from the 20th to 29th January, 1906, attended by a large number of sadhus and sashtris, under the Presidentship of Paramhansa Parivrajakacharya Jagadguru... of Govardhan Math". Sundaram has elaborately described the resolutions of the said Allahabad meeting first of which was[6]: "That a Hindu University be established at Benares under the name of the Bharatiya Vishwavidyalaya" (emphasis added). Other resolutions include objectives of promoting Sanatana Dharma, study of Sanskrit, and advancing scientific and technical knowledge through Sanskrit and Indian vernaculars[7]. It may be noted here that one does not find in Sundaram's account the names of those among whom the scheme of 1904 was circulated. The names of those who attended the 1905 meeting have also not been given. The *Sadhus and shastries* have of course been referred to as conspicuous, participants of Allahabad meeting of 1906. However, the Committee of the Vishwavidyalaya (formed in the meeting of 1906) remained virtually dormant. According to Malaviya himself[8] "... owing to circumstances which need not be mentioned here, an organized endeavour to carry out the proposal had to be put off year after year until last year" (1911).

Simultaneously, Sundaram writes[9]: "A number of Hindu gentlemen interested in the study of Hindu religion ... were considering proposal for the establishment of a high class educational institution at Banaras under the auspices of ..... the Hon'ble Maharaja Sir Rameshwar Singh Bahadur ... of Darbhanga". Rameshwara Singh had become the head of Darbhanga Raj after the death of his illustrious elder brother Lakshmishwara Singh in 1898.

2

Both the brothers were well educated (at Queen's College) and had acquired high proficiency in writing and speaking English as well as Sanskrit. After the death of his brother, Rameshwara Singh also came to be recognized as a very prominent national figure in political, economic and socio-cultural affairs both by the Government and people[10]. As the leading figure of the Bharat Dharma Mahamandala, he successfully organized Convention of Religions in Kolkata (1909) and Allahabad (1911). In his stress on the need of Hindu-Muslim unity, developing tolerance for one another and disapproved of the practice of untouchability[11] were widely appreciated. For example, one may see the reports published in The Empire, 20 April, 1910; The Indian Daily News, 17 April, 1910; The Bengalee, 17 April, 1910; The Statesman, 17 April, 1910; The Amrita Bazar Patrika, 25 April, 1910; Gnyanodaya (Bombay), 21 April, 1909, etc. However, his views for the abolition of untouchability and developing tolerance were intensely opposed by the strictly orthodox group of Hindus of Kolkata who even proposed to excommunicate him[12]. But, it seems that he was hardly shaken and held on to his mindset regarding Hinduism, rising above his zamindari (class) interests. He had also started thinking of establishing a university, Sri Sarda Visvavidyala in Banaras and published a booklet regarding his project around 1905 for circulation among prominent persons and educationists[13]. A copy of the prospectus of Sri Sarda Visvavidyalaya is given on Appendix 1. His ideas presented in his prospectus were, it seems, different from that of Malaviya (described before). He did not favour costly education. He emphasised on comparative study of Eastern and Western knowledge systems, English and Hindi, both to be adopted as the medium of instruction. Thus, three different projects were advanced simultaneously for establishing a University. The only common point was that the site for its establishment was Banaras. All considered this city to be the most prominent seat of higher education of different branches of learning since ancient days. Sundaram writes in this context that [14] "the distinguished persons as the head of these movements recognized this and decided to unite their forces and to work for a common Hindu University at Benares."

But, it seems that before the meeting of minds could take affect, Malaviya ignoring the schemes of others' began his movement in a manner that was considered questionable. An overview of his activities is given below. J.P. Hewett, lieutenant-Governor of the United Provinces (U.P.) wrote a letter to Harold Stuart, Secretary to the Government of India, Home Department, on 16 January,

1909 stating that he had received a letter along with some papers from Malaviya with a request to grant him approval and support to his proposal for establishing a Hindu University at Banaras. Hewett, however, made it clear in this letter that he was against establishing denominational universities in India[15].

Before this, on 10 December, 1909, Malaviya had written to the private secretary to His Honour the Lieutenant Governor of the United Provinces that [16] "towards the end of 1905 I put forward a proposal to establish a Hindu University at Banaras … the proposal was widely approved and I received several promises of support. But owing to causes, which it is not necessary to mention, I have not been able to push the idea forward. I intend shortly to resume work … to carry out the scheme…"(emphasis added). It is clear from his letter that until the end of 1908, there was no progress in this effort. In early 1909 (6 February), Sir Harold Stuart, Secretary to the Government of India, Home Department, wrote to J.P. Hewett (L.G., U.P) that the view that universities should be undenominational[17] "is one which commends itself to the Government of India…" (emphasis added). Thus, there was no hope of getting government approval of Malaviya's scheme. He, then, probably decided to rope in a very important ruling chief, Maharaja of Bikanir, to become the patron of the proposed university. Bikanir, however, made his stand clear to S.H. Butler. He wrote in his letter of May 9, 1911 to Butler that [18] "Pandit Madan Mohan Malaviya came to see me at Bombay … and asked me to be a Patron of the Hindu University … at Benares… I told him that I could support the movement only if it received the approval of Government,… I take it that the request of the Pandit to ask me to be a Patron was not merely a nominal thing but that he expects a couple of us chiefs at least to work energetically… I have already told the Pandit that personally I am not fond of advertising myself and that if I found that the Government favoured the scheme and approved of my taking any active part in the movement… even then he must get a bigger man… such as Scindia…" (emphasis added). It appears to be clear from above that for Bikanir too the approval of the Government was the precondition for his decision to be the patron of the scheme of the proposed university. Besides, he declared his policy of staying aloof from any kind of activism in this context ostensibly because he was "not fond of advertising" himself. Butler in his reply (23 August, 1911) to Bikanir mentioned that in fact there were three schemes of three different persons, namely, Malaviya, Mrs. Besant and the Maharaja of Darbhanga, and, further, he advised Bikanir as he had told Darbhanga not to do with any scheme without the approval of the Government[19].

Malaviya, it seems, having learnt the attitude of Bikanir, thought of utilizing Darbhanga. He, soon, began his tour of Bihar and Bengal for securing support for his scheme, Rameshwara Singh (hereafter to be referred as 'Darbhanga') in his letter of 28 August, 1911, wrote to Butler about Malaviya's plan to hold a meeting at Darbhanga in this context[20] and that "...he is giving out that his scheme has the support of Government". Butler in his letter of 31 August, 1911, to Du Boulay, wrote the following in this context[21]: "I forward Darbhanga's letter. I have heard from another source that Malaviya is taking the name of Government. Mrs. Besant did the same... I think the following communiqué might be issued:- 'It is understood that statements are being made to the effect that the Government of India are in sympathy with one or other of the proposals for a Hindu University which have been put forward. There is no foundation whatever for any such statement'." (emphasis added). However, Malaviya, it seems, remained undeterred and continued his activity. Darbhanga in his letter of 4 September, 1911, to Butler reported the following[22]: "He (Malaviya) has had meetings in Bankipur, Muzaffarpur and Darbhanga and was going to Bhagalpur and Calcutta... the Commissioner of the Division presided and the Collector attended the Muzaffarpur meeting and that the Collector of Darbhanga presided at the meeting at Darbhanga... Mr. Malaviya met me half an hour after the meeting was over. He said... I was not helping the movement and asked me to give him five lakhs at least. I replied that I could not help any scheme which had not Government approval... He warned me ...that I would lose all my public reputation if I failed to head the movement and give it full financial and other support." (emphasis added).

Reflecting on the events of Bankipur, Bhagalpur, etc., and Darbhanga's encounter with Malaviya (mentioned above) Shikha Chattopadhyaya (Mukherjee) comments that Darbhanga was[23] "...a man of weak personality and wholeheartedly supported the Hindu cause but at the same time devoted his all energy to earn the British patronage for selfish motive". It may be pointed out here that the Maharaja was not "a man of weak personality". It is not necessary to discuss here what sort of man was Darbhanga in detail. However, a few instances, for example, may be cited here to let the readers decide whether he was weak or courageous. In the deliberation of Indian Police Commission of 1902-03, he, as its only Indian member, gave a long note of dissent pleading strongly for the separation of judicial and executive functions and for recruitment of Indians also to higher ranks of Police administration[24]. Further, in 1909[25], "...

the free waters of the Ganges were in danger of being held up in Hardwar by the construction of a weir according to the Canal Scheme of the Government, he (Darbhanga) effectively demonstrated with the authorities... and had the Dam immediately opened and secured the free flow of water... to Saugor island". Further, to say that "he devoted his all energy to earn the British patronage for selfish motive" (stated by Sikha Chattopadhyaya (Mukherjee), mentioned above), seems to be a little far-fetched. In the context of establishing a denominational university in Banaras, he had no doubt in his mind that without British approval, no one at that time had the guts of advancing his/her scheme. Bikanir had also made it clear (mentioned before). So, earning British patronage was necessary. Under the circumstances, considering his effort and thinking as driven only by his "selfish motive", that is, his zamindari / class interests, it seems simply amounts to under estimating his intention and commitment.

Besides, Sikha Chattopadhyaya (Mukherjee) also writes that Darbhanga[26] "became very shaky by Malaviya's warning after the meeting". Maharaja had also referred to Malaviya's warning in his letter of 4 September, 1911, to Butler (mentioned before) she, further, writes on the basis of a report published in The Leader (28 September, 1911) that he (Darbhanga) was also embarrassed as the Dowager Maharanis (surviving wives of Lakshmeshwara Singh) supported Malaviya by contributing 12,000 rupees[27]. It may be mentioned here that according to Mahamahopadhyaya Dr. Sir Ganganatha Jha, an eminent contemporary of Rameshwara Singh, who was close to Darbhanga house, dowager Maharanis were not on good terms with him at that time, their relationship was rather one of intense conflict[28]. Malaviya, it seems, exploited this situation and managed successfully to approach the wives of Lakshmishwara Singh directly. Darbhanga might have been shocked at such a conduct of Malaviya. Besides, the participation of the British officers of the ranks of Commissioner and Collector in Malaviya's meetings held at Bhagalpur, Darbhanga, etc., (mentioned before), indicated in clear terms that they had been convinced by Malaviya's claim that his scheme had got the approval of the Government. Otherwise, how could such officers go to the extent of presiding over the meetings and consequently legitimizing Malaviya's stand? Darbhanga, instead of becoming "very shaky", might have been, perhaps, upset fearing that the paramount (colonial) power would not tolerate any false propaganda of its approval and would eventually react against any proposal. There was hardly any reason of his becoming "shaky" since there were quite a number of important persons in support of his leadership. For example, Maharaja of Tihri Gaurhwal having discussed the issue of Hindu University with a number of important Hindu leaders, expressed his trust and confidence in his leadership[29]. He, rightly considered the political leadership[30] that getting Government approval was necessary and for this it was essential to negotiate with the Colonial authorities regarding their terms and conditions. So, he wrote to Butler on 10 October, 1911, from Simla the following letter[30]:

Wheat-Field,

Simla

The 10" October, 1911

My Dear Mr. Butler,

You are aware that there is a widespread feeling amongst the Hindu public to establish a Hindu University on such lines as may be approved and sanctioned by the Government of India. More than one project has been put forward in this connection, but I think it very necessary, before any further action is taken in the direction of producing a complete scheme which will be generally acceptable to the Hindu public, that we should first try to obtain from you a clear indication of the lines on which Government will be prepared to support the idea of a Hindu University. I am quite convinced that Hindus will be only too happy to loyally carry out any directions that Government may be pleased to give them and will thankfully accept any suggestions that you may be pleased to make.

I hope that you will very kindly place this letter for the favourable consideration of His Excellency, the Viceroy.

Yours very sincerely,

(Sd)
Rameshwara Singh

Butler's reply (of 12 October, 1911) included a broad outline of the conditions for the grant of Government approval. The conditions implied a positive undertone recommending the steps that Muslims had taken so far for the proposed university in Aligarh. The text of the letter is given below[31]:

Simla

The 12th October, 1911.

My dear Maharaja Bahadur,

I have received your letter of the 10th instant in which you refer to the wide-spread movement amongst the Hindu public to establish a Hindu University on such lines as may be approved and sanctioned by the Government of India, to the different schemes put forward, and to the desirability of my making a pronouncement as to the lines on which Government will be prepared to support the idea of a Hindu University. You add that you are quite convinced that Hindus will be only too happy to carry out loyally any directions that Government may be pleased to give them and will thankfully accept any suggestion that I may be pleased to make.'

You will understand that in the absence of definite and detailed schemes it is not possible for me at present to do more than indicate certain conditions, on which the Government of India must insist as antecedent to the recognition by Government of a movement for the establishment of a Hindu University. These are:-

(1) The Hindus should approach Government in a body as the Mohammadans did;

(2) A strong efficient and financially sound college with an adequate European staff should be the basis of the Scheme;

(3)   The University should be a modern University, mainly in being a teaching and residential University and offering religious instruction;

(4)   The movement should be entirely educational;

(5)   There should be the same measure of Government supervision and opportunity to give advice as in the case of the proposed University at Aligarh.

I need scarcely add that it would be necessary hereafter to satisfy the Government of India and the Secretary of State as to the adequacy of the funds collected and the suitability in all particulars of the constitution of the University. The Government of India must of course reserve to itself full power in regard to all details of any scheme which they may hereafter place before the Secretary of State, whose discretion in regard to the movement and any proposals that may arise from it, they cannot in any way prejudice.

I may add that the Government of India appreciate the spirit of the concluding passage of your letter and that **you can count on the ungrudging co-operation of myself and the department** (emphasis added) in furthering any scheme that may commend itself to the Government of India and the Secretary of State.

Yours sincerely,

(Sd)

Harcourt Butler.

Considering Butler's attitude quite positive and encouraging, Darbhanga now, decided to launch his activity to make the project a success. He also made a very handsome donation of Rupees Five lakh to the proposed university[32]. The first public meeting was, then, held at Meerut. The deputation to this town, headed by Darbhanga[33] "was received very enthusiastically by the people there. He presided over the Meerut meeting, held on 17 October, 1911, and delivered his presidential speech. In his address, he said that he had made it clear to Malaviya (in July, 1911) that he would begin to work for securing public support after receiving Government assurance. He also mentioned that in his meeting with Malaviya, it was <u>decided that he (Maharaja) should approach the Government and ascertain its</u> views. Malaviya, who had warned him before that he would lose his reputation because of not supporting his (Malaviya's) scheme, it seems, now reconciled to the reality. The details of the text of his presidential address are given below[34]:

**At a Public meeting in connection with the
Hindu University held at Meerut
on 17th October 1911
H.H. the Maharaja Bahadur of Darbhanga who occupied
the chair said:-**

Gentlemen I heartily thank you for the cordial reception you have accorded to me and the members of the Hindu University deputation and for the honour you have done me in asking to Preside at this gathering. The question of a Hindu University has long been in the air. Many years ago the idea presented itself to the Bharata Dharma Mahamandala.... However ... it was absolutely necessary to get some indication of the wishes of Government on the Subject.

2.... Our lasting gratitude is due to His Excellency the Viceroy and to the Hon'ble Member for Education for the very kindly personal interest which they have taken in the matter. I shall have the pleasure of laying before you the correspondence that has passed between me and the Hon'ble Mr. Butler and I am convinced that you will consider it eminently satisfactory. He has most kindly agreed to receive a deputation at Delhi after his return from Bombay when we are to discuss informally the details of the scheme with him. I understand that the Hindu University will not identify itself with any sect or creed ... I hold that an education which does not provide for instruction in the religion of one's forefathers can never be complete and am convinced that a Hindu will be a better

Hindu, a Christian a better Christian, and a Mohammedan a better Mohammadan, if he has implicit faith in his God and the religion of his forefathers. I have never believed in a godless education and have invariably advocated the necessity of combining secular education with religious training. I join in the movement for the University in the earnest hope that it will produce this happy combination and that the boys whom it shall turn out will be God-loving, truthful, loyal to their Sovereign, devoted to their country, and fit in every way to take their place in the great future that lies before them.

Bhagavan Das writes in this context in his article,[35] "However, after much difficulty and discussion in the public press, caused by the vagaries going on within the CHC and elsewhere, certain conditions were agreed upon in writing, as below, between the promoters of the Hindu University on the one hand and Mrs. Besant on the other, on 22nd October, 1911. The conditions were:

1. That the name of the University shall be the Hindu University.
2. That the first governing body shall consist of representatives of the Hindu Community and Mrs. Besant and representative Trustees of the Central Hindu College.
3. That the Theological faculty shall be entirely in the hands of the Hindus.
4. That the petition for a charter now before the Secretary of State for India shall be withdrawn."

According to V.A. Sundaram[36], "On the 22nd October, 1911, the Hon'ble Maharaja Sir Rameshwara Singh Bahadur, K.C.I.E., of Darbhanga, Mrs. Annie Besant and the Hon'ble Pandit Madan Mohan Malaviya and a few other gentlemen met at Benaras. The conclusions then arrived at are embodied in the following short memorandum, which was then drawn up:-

1. That the name of the University shall be the Hindu University.
2. That the first governing body shall consist of representatives of the Hindu Community and Mrs. Besant and representative Trustees of the Central Hindu College.
3. That the Theological faculty shall be entirely in the hands of the Hindus.

4. That the petition for a charter now before the Secretary of State for India shall be withdrawn.

(Sd.) Rameshwara Singh

(Sd.) Annie Besant

(Sd.) Madan Mohan Malaviya

(Sd.) Sundar Lal

(Sd.) Ganga Prasad Verma

(Sd.) Bhagwan Das

(Sd.) Iswar Saran".

Subsequently, Darbhanga wrote to Butler on 31 October, 1911, that[37]

"Mrs. Besant grasped the situation at once. I saw Pandit Sundar Lal at Benares but could get no opportunity to have a private talk with him. I am afraid however that you will have some difficulty in getting him to fall in with your views. Sir John Hewett was not very sure about his willingness. However there is plenty of time to think about the question and I have no doubt that matters will be all right in the end.

Malaviya writes to me to accompany a delegation to Bikanir and Gwalior. I am writing to him that it will be best to wait till after the Delhi Darbar. I have also written to His Highness Bikanir to the same effect. I think that it will be just as well if the Chiefs were to join after you have an opportunity of talking to him.

I have received several suggestions to the effect that it will be an excellent thing if His Majesty were to say a few words expressing his pleasure at the inception of the two Universities. Personally I am sure that Hindus and Mohemdans will be delighted at such an expression of His Majesty's opinion. May I suggest that you could mention the subject to His Excellency if you agree with me...

I was told in Benaras that the 2ⁿᵈ and 5ᵗʰ Dec. would suit them better than the 30ᵗʰ November............ kindly let me have a wire. Would you wire to me to send me a list of the members that they propose to form the Deputation.

Please send to me any suggestions on university that you may consider necessary and I will do my best to ...."

He again wrote the following to Butler on 8 Novermber, 1911, thanking him for his efforts for convincing Sir Sundar Lal to become the Secretary of the proposed Society for the establishment of the University[38]:

"I thought it would be really a difficult matter but was sure that you would be able to do it and was not surprised when I received Malaviya's telegram, at the same time that I received your letter, to the effect that Sundar Lal had accepted the Secretaryship. I have nothing now but to proceed forward. I see that you have agreed to the 3ʳᵈ December being the date of the deputation. I have told Malaviya that Chiefs are to come into the scheme after the deputation was over. He wanted me to go to Bikanir and Gwalior on deputation but both the Maharaja and myself have advised him to postpone and till after His Majesty leaves India."

Then according to Sundaram[39]: "On the 22ⁿᵈ October, 1911, the Hon'ble Maharaja Sir Rameshwara Singh Bahadur, K.C.I.E. of Darbhanga, Mrs. Annie Besant and the Hon'ble Pandit Madan Mohan Malaviya and a few other gentlemen met at Benares. The conclusions then arrived at are embodied in the following short memorandum, which was then drawn up:
1. That the name of the University shall be the Hindu University.
2. That the first governing body shall consist of representatives of the Hindu community and Mrs. Annie Besant and representative Trustees of the Central Hindu Collage.
3. That the theological faculty shall be entirely in the hands of the Hindus.
4. That the petition for a Charter now before the Secretary of State for India shall be withdrawn.

Signed by Rameshwara Singh, Annie Besant, Madan Mohn Malaviya, Sundar lal, Ganga Prasad Verma.

Thereafter, a meeting of a large number of persons representing Hindu elites was held in Allahabad on 28 November, 1911, under the Chairmanship of Darbhanga. Sundaram describes in detail the deliberation held in this meeting in the following words[40]: "...The outlines of the constitution... were revised. It was further decided in the same meeting that a deputation of the Hindu community headed by the Hon'ble Maharaja Sir Rameshwara Singh Bahadur, K.C.I.E., of Darbhanga, should wait upon the Hon'ble Member for Education at Delhi. The Hon'ble Sir Harcourt Butler readily expressed his willingness to receive the deputation which consisted of the following gentlemen:-

1. The Hon'ble Maharaja Sir Rameshwara Singh, Bahadur, K.C.I.E., of Darbhanga
2. Mrs. Annie Besant
3. The Hon'ble Pandit Madan Mohan Malaviya
4. The Hon'ble Dr. Sundar Lal, C.I.E., Allahabad
5. The Hon'ble Maharaja Mahindra Chandra Nundy of Cossimbazar
6. Mr. V.P. Madhava Rao, C.I.E., ex-Dewan of Mysore
7. The Hon'ble Mr. N.Subba Rao Pantulu, Madras.
8. The Hon. Mr. Harchandrai Vishindas of Karachi
9. The Hon. Rai Shadi Lal Bahadur, Lahore
10. Lala Harkishen Lal, Lahore
11. The Hon. Rai Bahadur Lala Hari Chand, Multan
12. The Hon. Lala Sultan Singh, Delhi
13. The Hon. Baba Guru Baksha Singh Bedi, Punjab
14. The Hon. Maharaja Sir Bhagwati Prasad Singh K.C.I.E., of Balrampur, Oudh
15. The Hon. Rana Sir Sheoraj Singh, K.C.I.E., of Khajurgaon
16. The Hon. Raja Rampal Singh, C.I.E., Kurri Sidhauli, Oudh
17. The Hon. Rai Ganga Prasad Varma Bahadur, Lucknow
18. The Hon. Rai Sri Ram Bahadur, C.I.E., Lucknow
19. The Hon. Lala Sukhbir Sinha, Muzaffarnagar
20. The Hon. Babu Moti Chand, Benaras
21. Mahamahopadhyaya Pandit Siva Kumar Sastri, Benaras
22. Pandit Gokaran Nath Misra, Lucknow
23. Rai Bahadur Pandit Maharaj Narayan Sivapuri, Benaras

24. The Hon. Rai Ram Saran Dass Bahadur, Lahore
25. The Mahant of Tarkeshwar
26. Rai Badri Das Bahadur, Mukeem, Calcutta
27. Babu Bhagwan Das, Benaras
28. Mahamahopadhyaya Bankey Lal Nawal Goswami, Delhi
29. Rao Bahadur V.N. Pandit, Napur
30. Maharja Girija Nath Roy Bahadur of Dinajpur
31. Pandi Din Dayal Sharma, Rohtak
32. Sir Pratul ChandraChatterji, Kt. C.I.E, Lahore.

It seems that the list of persons (32 in number) included in the proposed Deputation mentioned by Sundaram (given above) was incomplete. Darbhanga informed Butler (while both of them were at Coronation Durbar Camp, Delhi, at the time) on 30 November, 1911, that Babu Langat Singh (of Muzaffarpur, Bihar), whose name was 36th on the list, had shown his willingness to join the Deputation[41]. The Deputation was formally[42] "received by the Hon'ble Member for Education in the Town Hall of Delhi on 4 December, 1911. The draft constitution of the university was presented for the consideration and advice of …Butler. Several points were…. discussed… great sympathy and support… he accorded… throughout". Soon, a meeting was held in Delhi and, according to Sundaram[43], "…it was decided to begin work under the auspices of the Hindu University Society at once. An office was opened at Allahabad on the 1st January, 1912.". Sundaram mentions the following names who constituted the Committee of Management[44]:

1. **President**: The Hon'ble Maharaja Sir Rameshwara Singh Bahadur, K.C.I.E., of Darbhanga
2. **Vice-President**: Sir Gooroodass Banerji, Kt., Calcutta
3. **Vice-President**: Mrs. Annie Besant, President of the Board of Trustees, Central Hindu College, Benaras
4. **Vice-President**: Dr. Rash Behari Ghosh, C.S.I., C.I.E, Calcutta
5. **Honorary Secretary**: The Hon'ble Pandit Sundar Lal, Rai Bahadur, B.A., C.I.E., LL.D., Allahabad
6. The Hon'ble Maharaja Manindra Chandra Nundy Bahadur, Cossimbazar, Murshidabad
7. Babu Brajendra Kishore Roy Chowdhry, Calcutta
8. The Hon'ble Mr. Justice, A. Chaudhuri, Calcutta

9. Babu Hirendranath Datta, M.A., Calcutta
10. Professor Radha Kumud Mukherji, M.A., Calcutta
11. Professor Benoy Kumar Sarkar, M.A., Calcutta
12. The Hon'ble Kuar Krityanand Sinha, Bareilly, Purneah
13. The Hon'ble Babu Braja Kishore Prasad, Vakil, Laheria-Sarai
14. The Hon'ble Babu Krishna Sahai, Vakil, Bankipur
15. Seth Radha Krishna Potdar, Calcutta
16. Babu Langat Singh, Zamindar, Muzaffarpore
17. Rai Purnendu Narain Sinha, Bahadur, M.A., B.L., Vakil, Bankipur
18. The Hon'ble Mr. N. Subba Rao, Rajahmundry
19. The Hon'ble Mr. L.A. Govind Raghava Iyer, Madras
20. The Hon'ble Mr. T.V. Seshagiri Iyer, Vakil, Madras
21. Mr. V.P. Madhava Rao, C.I.E., Ex-Dewan of Mysore, Bangalore
22. The Hon'ble Sir Vithal Das Thackersay, Bombay
23. Sir Bhalchandra Krishna Bhatwadekar, Bombay
24. The Hon'ble Mr. Gokul Das Parekh, Bombay
25. Mr. Dharamsey Morarjee Gokul Das, Bombay
26. The Hon'ble Mr. Harchandrai Vishindas, Karachi
27. Mr. V.R. Pandit, Bar-at-Law, Nagpur
28. Rao Bahadur Vaman Rao Kolhatkar, Nagpur
29. The Hon'ble Mr. R.N. Mudholkar, Amraoti
30. Rai Bahadur Lala Lalchand, Lahore
31. Rai Ram Saran Das Bahadur, Lahore
32. Mr. Harkishen Lal, Bar-at-Law, Lahore
33. The Hon'ble Rai Hari Chand Bahadur, Multan
34. The Hon'ble Lala Sultan Singh, Delhi
35. Sirdar Jogendra Singh, Home Member, Patiala State
36. Pandit Din Dayal Sharma, Jhajjur, Rohtak
37. Raja Munshi Madho Lal, C.S.I., Benaras
38. Mahamahopadhyaya Pandit Adityara Bhattacharya, M.A., Allahabad
39. The Hon'ble Raja Rampal Singh, C.I.E., of Kurri Sidhauli, Rae Bareli
40. The Hon'ble Rai Ganga Prasad Varma Bahadur, Lucknow
41. The Hon'ble Rai Sri Ram Bahadur, C.I.E., Lucknow
42. Thakur Suraj Bux Singh, Taluqdar, Kasmanda, Sitapur
43. The Hon'ble Babu Brijnandan Prasad, M.A., LL.B., Moradabad
44. The Hon'ble Lala Sukhbir Sinha, Muzaffarnagar

45. Rai Prag Narayan Bhargava Bahadur, Lucknow
46. Rai Ram Sarandas Bahadur, Manager, The Oudh Commercial Bank, Ld., Faizabad
47. Babu Vikramjit Singh, B.A., LL.B., Cawnpore
48. Babu Moti Chand, Benaras
49. Rai Krishnaji, Benaras
50. Rao Gopal Das Sahpuri, Benaras
51. Babu Gauri Shanker Prasad, B.A., LL.B., Benaras
52. Pandit Baldev Ram dave, Vakil, Allahabad
53. Dr. Satish Chandra Banerji, M.A., LL.D., Allahabad
54. Dr. Tej Bahadur Sapru, M.A., LL.D., Allahabad
55. Babu Iswar saran, B.A., LL.B., Allahabad
56. The Hon'ble Pandit Madan Mohan Malaviya, B.A., LL.B., Allahabad
57. Babu Bhagavan Das, M.A., Benaras
58. Pandit Gokaran Nath Misra, M.A., LL.B., Vakil, Lucknow
59. Pandit Krishnaram Mehta, B.A., LL.B., Vakil, Benaras
60. Rai Iqbal Narain Gurtu, M.A., LL.B., Benaras
61. Babu Mangla Prasad, M.A., Benaras

It seems to be quite significant to note that the Committee consisted of such intellectuals as Professor Radha Kumud Mukherji, Professor Benoy Kumar Sarkar, Bhagvan Das, Mm. Aditya Ram Bhattacharya, etc., eminent lawyers such as Tej Bahadur Sapru, Gokaran Nath Mishra and others, and prominent persons from different regions of the country. Darbhanga was made the President and Gooroodass Banerji and Mrs. Besant were made Vice-Presidents, Sundar Lal was made the Secretary of this Committee. Malaviya's name appears on the list only as a member of the Committee.

Notes:

1. Misra, B.B. 1961 The Indian Middle Class, London, New York, Bombay, Oxford University Press, p.283
2. Chatterjee, Partha 1993 The Nation and Its Fragments; Colonial and Postcolonial Histories, Princeton, New Jersey, Princeton University Press, p.26
3. Ibid, p.120
4. Sundaram, V.A. 1936 Benaras Hindu University 1905 to 1935, Benaras, Tara Printing Works, p.80

5. Ibid, p.I
6. Ibid, p.II
7. Ibid, pp Ii-IV
8. Ibid, p.2
9. Ibid, p.80
10. For details in this context, see Jha, Hetukar ed.2010 A Liberal Aristocrat, Maharajadhiraja Rameshwara Singh of Darbhanga (1860-1929), Kameshwar Singh Bihar Heritage Series-14, Darbhanga, (Bihar), Maharajadhiraja Kameshwar Singh Kalyani Foundation. (henceforth Kalyani Foundation).
11. His speeches and press reports have been published. See Jha, Hetukar ed. 2010 A Liberal Aristocrat, Maharajadhiraja Rameshwara Singh of Darbhanga (1860-1929), pp36-57
12. The entire proceedings of the meeting of the strictly orthodox group held in Kolkata have been published. See Jha, Hetukar ed 2010 A Liberal Aristocrat: Maharajadhiraja Rameshwara Singh of Darbhanga (1860-1929), pp. 55-57
13. Sundaram, op.cit, p.80
14. Ibid, pp 80-81
15. Ghosh, Suresh Chandra ed. 1977 Development of University Education 1916-1920, Selections From Educational Records of the Government of India, Volume II, New Delhi, Jawaharlal Nehru University, p.29
16. Ibid, p.30
17. Ibid, p.32
18. Ibid, pp 32-33
19. Ibid, p.34
20. Ibid. pp. 35-36
21. Ibid, pp.36-37
22. Ibid, p.38
23. Chattopadhyaya (Mukherjee), Sikha, 1980 Besant, Malaviya, The Maharaja of Darbhanga, The Emergence of the Banaras Hindu University, The First Denominational University of India, New Delhi: Ph.D. Thesis, Zakir Husain Centre for Educational Studies, Jawaharlal Nehru University, p.322
24. See the text of Maharaja's Dissent in Jha, Hetukar ed. 2010, op.cit, pp.157-164

25. See The Maharaja of Darbhanga, An Appreciation, 1916, Madras, Ganesh & Co., p.11. The entire text has been included in Jha, Hetukar ed.2010, op.cit. pp 298-306

26. Chattopadhyaya (Mukherjee), Sikha, op.cit., p.325

27. Ibid, p.325

28. See in this context Jha, Hetukar ed 1976 Autobiographical Notes of Mahamahopadhyaya Dr. Sir Ganganatha Jha, The Journal of the Ganganatha Jha Sanskrit Vidyapeetha, Vol. XXX, Parts (1-4), 1974, Allahabad, pp 41-42

29. See Gaurhwal's letter of 16 September, 1911, This letter is preserved in the Archives of Kalyani Foundation. A scanned copy of this letter is given on Appendix-2

30. See Sundaram, op.cit., p.83

31. Ibid, pp.84-85

32. Ibid, p.86

33. Ibid, p.86

34. A copy of this address is preserved in Kalyani Foundation archives. A scanned copy has been given on Appendix-3

35. Bhagavan Das published a pamphlet entitled: The Central Hindu College and Mrs. Besant, from London in 1913. The entire text of this pamphlet has been reprinted and included in Jha, Hetukar ed 2010, op.cit., pp 2-16. It is in this pamphlet that he described the event of 22nd October, 1911, pp 6-7

36. Sundaram, V.A., op.cit, pp 86-87

37. See File no. MSS EUR F116/70 British Libraries, London

38. Ibid, A copy of it is also available in Kalyani Foundation archive, a scanned copy of this letter is given on Appendix 5

39. Sundaram, V.A., op.cit, pp 86-87

40. Ibid, pp 87-89

41. See File No. MSS EUR F116/70, British Libraries, London

42. Sundaram, V.A., op.cit, pp 89-90

43. Ibid, p.90

44. Ibid, pp 90-93

Chapter 2

Hindu University Society and the Establishment of Banaras Hindu University

About the events which occurred after 1 January, 1912, Sundaram writes that the Society soon took up the task of preparing a list of the names of those who had promised to give donations[1]. He, further, mentions that four meetings of the Committee were held and the Deputation of Hindu University visited the following places[2]: Kheri, Fyzabad, Jaunpur, Bankipur, Gorakhpur, Cawnpore, Capra, Mozufferpur, Darbhanga, Bhagalpur, Monghyr, Lucknow, Calcutta, Faridabad, Malda, Rawalpindi, Lahore, Amritsar, Muzaffarnagar, Meerut, Bareily, Saharanpur, Moradabad, Unao, Sitapur, Etawah, Bahraich, Benaras, Agra, Ajmere, Udaipur, Naini Tal, Almora, Kashmir, Ambala, Simla, Rai Bareli, Indore and Kotah.

However, one does not find in his account when and where the (above mentioned) four meetings were held, how the Deputations were constituted and who were the members of the said Deputations. He, then, refers to[3] "Large meetings at Calcutta and many other places" addressed by Malaviya, one of which had been presided over by Bikanir. However, the name of Darbhanga, who was the President of the Society, has not been mentioned in this context, nor is there any text of Malaviya's speech available in Sundaram's book. Bikanir had written a letter to Butler on 12 January, 1912, informing him about the invitation from the Society for Hindu University to preside over the meeting to be held on 17 January, 1912, at the Town Hall, Calcutta. He sought suggestion regarding what he would say in his speech[4]. Subsequently, the meeting was held at Calcutta Town Hall on 17 January, 1912. A document (preserved in the Kalyani Foundation Archives) throws much light on the deliberation of the said meeting. According to it, Darbhanga, president of the Society, proposed the name of Bikanir to preside over the meeting and introduced him to the audience. Then with due permission of the Chair, he delivered a speech on the scheme of the university and work done till then as well as the future plan[5]:A few important points are given below:

> "Your Highness and Gentlemen, We are met this afternoon as, you are all aware, to promote the scheme for the establishment of a Hindu University for the whole of India. ---. The Government have approved of the erection of a Hindu University and it is along the lines which they have indicated that we are now proceeding and venture to hope that success will ultimately crown our efforts backed, as we know they will be, by the sympathetic co-operation of the enlightened opinion of all the various sections of our community.

> The noble and inspiring reply of the King-Emperor to the University Deputation on Saturday, 6th January last, ought to send a thrill of hope through the breasts of every educationist in the land. I make no apology for quoting His Majesty's words. He said: "It is to the Universities of India that I look to assist in that gradual union and fusion of the culture and aspirations of Europeans and Indians on which the future well-being of India so greatly depends". And again, "you have to conserve the ancient learning and simultaneously to push forward Western Science. You have also to build up character without which learning is of little value". These words of wisdom surely ring out the death-knell of a godless education,

for character can only be built up in so far as it is deeply rooted in the religious life.

In another paragraph of his reply, the King Emperor said: "Today in India I give to India the watchword of hope. On every side I trace the signs and strivings of new life. Education has given you hope, and through better and higher education, you will build up higher and better hopes." With these words ringing in our ears we cannot do otherwise than press forward with enthusiasm to the realization of our scheme for a Hindu University for India.

The question of funds is a problem which we will have to solve. We have already received subscriptions amounting to Rs.43 lakhs, which mark a beginning, and which I trust will prove but the earnest of the three crores which, at least, will be required before a thoroughly equipped University can claim to be of the same rank as those in Europe. But I believe that with enthusiasm through all the ranks of our community in India, condensed into fruitful channels of liberality, the money will not be wanting in due time for the fulfillment of our wishes, and for landing the proposed University into the realm of achievement.

The work of a University, as I take it, is for the development of a student into his true manhood – to make him an all-round good man,

We rejoice to think that our Mahomedan countrymen are similarly engaged in promoting a Mahomedan University at Aligarh, the seat of Mahomedan learning, under the leadership of my friend H.H. the Agha Khan, and we wish them all success in their enterprise. They, too, believe with ourselves that only as the intellectual is penetrated with spiritual life, so only can their youths be fitted to take their true place in the social and political realm as men of wide culture and true patriotism.

I hope and trust that the scheme on which we have embarked will be taken up with enthusiasm, by every Hindu who has the moral regeneration and the intellectual uplift of his people at heart – an enthusiasm which nothing will be allowed to damp until the object of our ardent desire is fully accomplished. Then shall India begin to take her true place amongst the Nations of the world. God speed the day."

In his presidential speech, Darbhanga revealed his comprehensive vision of the university of denominational nature without being sectarian. He did not ignore the names of Mrs. Besant and Malaviya in his speech in any context. He also mentioned the names of his eminent Muslim friends such as H.H. Agha Khan, the Raja of Jahagirabad, Mr. Justice Rahim, Mr. Hasan Imam and others who had extended their cooperation and support to the Hindu University project and pointed out that Hindus had also responded similarly to their feelings. He pointed out in clear terms that "The Government of India in their cordial approval of the schemes of Mahomedan and Hindu Universities, know... the unifying effect of such institutions in the promotion of kindly feelings...". Besides, he quite analytically discussed the objectives, nature and scope of the university.

On 21st February, 1912, Bikanir wrote[6] to Butler stating that he had received a letter from Darbhanga, saying that he had received an unfavourable reply from Mysore and therefore he (Darbhanga) proposed the name of the Hon'ble Maharaja of Jammu and Kashmir. He further said that he did not want a dummy or a figure head but a chief who will work heart and soul for and be of real use to the University. Sir James Du Boulay wrote[7] from the Government House Simla to Sir Butler on 26 February, 1912, that His Excellency did quite agree with the advice from Maharaja of Darbhanga on the issue of Patronship.

Soon, on 27 February, 1912, Butler replied to Bikanir. He wrote[8] that:

"I knew Durbhunga had that proposal in mind, and advised him to consult Your Highness about it and, if you did not agree, as I thought you probably might not, to leave the patronship open for the present. It is not altogether desirable that you should publish Mysore's refusal. And although the terms of his letter preclude a further reference to him now, later on there may be means

of inducing him to change his mind. At any rate it is well to leave things open."

In reply to this letter, Bikanir wrote on 11 March, 1912, thanking him for his advice and mentioned the following[9]:

"I am writing to Durbhunga to try and let him move away from his place and to come with the deputation to Rajputana. I am sure it would be a good thing. Unless the deputation visits the states nothing much can be done in the way of their subscribing. All I can do is to work up a bit by writing to the Chief whom I know well and thus have the way."

As advised by Bikanir and Butler, Darbhanga, it seems, decided to pursue his programme of leading the Deputation to every prospective big donor and the Ruling Chiefs across the country.

On 11 April, 1912, Malaviya wrote to Darbhanga requesting him to instruct his manager to circulate a notice to the employees of Raj Darbhanga, asking them for donations out of free-will[10], Darbhanga sent a letter to his General Manager who dispatched a circular to the Circle Managers[11].

Darbhanga had called a meeting at Allahabad of Muslim leaders in 1910 and again on 1 January, 1912. H.H. Agha Khan presided over both the meetings. The issue was to resolve the difference between Muslims and Hindus regarding Hindu University[12]. The Hon'ble Aga Khan donated Rs. 10,000 to the Hindu University. Darbhanga was invited to visit Aligarh. He went to Aligarh on 13 June 1912, explained his views and contributed Rs.20,000/- to the Muslim University Fund[13].

On 15 June, 1912, Darbhanga wrote the following to Butler from Lahore[14]:

"Very many thanks for your letter. I will try to interest the Maharaja of Kashmir. Will you kindly suggest how I can approach Indore who I hear has come to Kashmir. I knew his father very well but do not know him .... **Malaviya is at Almora.**

He again wrote to Butler on 28 June, 1912, about the success of the Kashmir Deputation in the following words[15]:

"I have been detained here longer than I expected. In a native state things do not go at railway speed. The Darbar will not be able to air a donation at present but hopes to make an announcement next year. At present an annual subscription of Rs.12000/- will be announced at a meeting to be held on Monday next. The Resident told me that … he had modified his views after a formal appeal from me. I could not find Indore. He has been out bear shooting and I did not think it would serve any useful purpose if I followed him. I hear that the Maharajas of Gwalior and Bikaner are to be in Simla very shortly. I have asked Sir James to remind H.E. about speaking to Maharaja Scindia and shall be much obliged if you will also kindly help…

The University meeting is to take place on the 1st July. I leave the next day and arrive at Salone on the 5th and Simla in the afternoon of the 6th…. I shall try to see you on my way from the railway station if you will kindly drop me a line to meet me…"

On 5 July, 1912, Darbhanga wrote to Butler from Lahore stating[16] that:

"…the Kashmir Darbar will with the advise of the Resident give Rs.12000/- a year which capitalized amounts to Three lakhs. The Kashmir Chief Minister will give an annuity in capitalized value of which will amount to thirty to thirty five thousand. The other subscriptions were about twenty thousand. The quantum of a donation will be considered in next year's budget…

I saw Holkar. He told me he would be glad to help.

I shall be much obliged if you could speak to His Highness of Goalier (Gwalior)..."

On 10 July, 1912, he (Darbhanga) wrote in a private letter to Butler that [17]

"I have already spoken to you about Maharaja Scindia but I forgot to speak about Patiala. I am told His Highness is already in Simla and now you will very kindly help in that direction also. I told you that Maharaja Holkar promised me that he would help and that he invited me in the cold weather to Indore..."

On 19 July, 1912, Sundar Lal wrote the following letter[18] to Darbhanga:

"I am glad to acknowledge the receipt of your reply dated 17th July 1912 and with it of the report on the proceedings of the meeting held in Kashmir and of the list of the donations given. **The report is interesting reading and is a valuable contribution to the literature of the Hindu University movement. My office has made copies both of the report and of the list and they are, in accordance with your desire, returned to you.**

I hope to see some mention of the work done by Your Highness in connection with the Hindu University movement in the Resume, I am expecting from the Hon'ble Pandit Madan Mohan Malaviya. The hints given of your independent activity are additional points and they will of course find a place in the six-monthly report." (emphasis added)

In his letter, Sundar Lal referred to a <u>report</u> on Kashmir Deputation and considered it to be "a valuable contribution to the literature of the Hindu University movement", perhaps, for its (report's) detailed coverage of the enthusiastic reception (accorded to the Deputation) and donation of more than 118 persons, besides that of Maharaja and other important authorities of Kashmir. However, he simply hoped to "see <u>some</u> mention of the work done" by Darbhanga in the Resume that he was expecting from Malaviya. Besides, it is difficult to understand what Sundar Lal meant by referring to his "independent activity". All his activities for the University were, in fact, those of Darbhanga as the President of the Society. Sundar Lal's letter seems to suggest implicitly that Darbhanga's efforts were not being taken note of properly by those who were responsible for preparing six-monthly reports. Parts of the full text of the Kashmir report are given below[19]:

"The Hindu University Deputation in Kashmir
1ˢᵗ July, 1912

Yesterday (July the first) must be regarded as one of the most memorable days in the history of modern Kashmir. For it was yesterday that witnessed a great and noble act performed by its ruler who was joined in it loyally and in full and hearty co-operation by all his subjects and servants, Hindu and Mussalmans even though the act performed concerned chiefly the Hindu community of which His Highness the Maharaja Sahib Bahadur of Kashmir is both an ornament and one of the principal leaders. This act consisted in His Highness' making an announcement, in a great public meeting and in response to a touching appeal made by the Hon'ble the Maharaja Sahib Bahadur of Darbhanga, of His Highness' contribution to the Hindu University movement which has now for over two years been so powerfully moving the Hindu Community in all its sections in all parts of the country. The deed and the occasion were unique not only for the noble gift which His Highness the Maharaja Sahib made to the Hindu University but for the spirit by which the whole of the proceedings were animated and all present were dominated. For it was a spirit of love and brotherliness, not only among the Hindus present but between these on the one hand and the Muhamedan subjects and servants of His Highness as a body on the other and a spirit of united loyalty and devotion on the part of both the community to the throne and person of His Gracious and

Imperial Majesty the King and Emperor as representing the Divine Ruling Power,...

Deeply moved as the assembly was by the persuasive eloquence of Pandit Din Dayal, it had now the privilege of listening to the touching appeal which the **Maharaja Bahadur of Darbhanga addressed in Hindi to His Highness of Kashmir**, his Chief Minister, the other ministers and servants of His Highness and to the general public....

I am a Brahmin and it has been the practice of the Brahmins of old to beg. And although I have not been personally in the habit of begging before, I still come before you in the capacity of a mendicant and I hope and trust that you will give with your whole heart and soul, so that I may be encouraged in my new profession, and that I may not go away empty handed to be laughed at by the public....

To this appeal His Highness the Maharaja Sahib Bahadur of Kashmir replied...

"Maharaja Sahib of Darbhanga... is here in connection with the Hindu University movement. I am sorry his stay is going to be very short. He has, you will be glad to learn, been gazetted as a member of the Executive Council of Behar. We should be grateful to the Imperial Government for having conferred this honour upon one who is the leader of the Hindu Community as represented by the Dharma Mahamandala. It is a happy sign – which betokens marvelous progress that has been made – that it has become possible for Raises to meet together. In olden times, the Raises could not meet. They could not join even socially one with the other.

... I have every hope that the Maharaja will take permission of the Government of India to see his life-work fulfilled and steer the ship clear of the shoals and pitfalls – for there is no one else who wields so great an influence with the aristocracy and the middle classes which the Maharaja wields alike by his wealth, education and religious principles. It is fortunate, gentlemen, that the movement should have been started under so high auspices....

I am happy that my subjects both Hindu and Muhamedan have mustered so strong to day. Their appearing together to further the cause which this movement has in view establishes that they are one in sympathy and ideals.

... The Report further includes the following:

His Highness was followed by his Chief Minister who,... announced the gift of His Highness in the following words :-

"His Highness the Maharaja Sahib Bahadur has commanded me to announce on his behalf that he very generously grants for ever from the State Treasury Rs.1000/- a month (i.e.Rs.12000/- a year) as an aid to the Hindu University....

His Highness has further ordered me to declare that he will constantly bear in mind the needs of the Hindu University as it advances on practical lines and would make occasional grants and donations in future as well."

This announcement, which really means, apart from promises of future donations, a present gift of Rs. 3,50,000/- being the capitalized value of the annual grant of Rs. 12000/- was received with great cheers and the Maharaja Bahadur of Darbhanga acknowledged it with thanks.

Then came an appeal to the officials and Raises of the State and the general public, again by Pandit Din Dayal speaking on behalf of the Maharja Bahadur of Darbhanga. And in response, there came promises and announcements from all sides of the gathering, the Muhammedans vying with the Hindus in their alacrity to contribute.

Of these gifts, one of Rs.5000/- was promised on behalf of Raj Kumar Shri Hari Singh Sahib and another of Rs.2000/- on that of Maharajakumar Jagatdev Singh, the adopted son of His Highness the Maharaja Sahib Bahadur.

The gift of the Chief Minister Rai Sahib Diwan Amar Nath Sahib C.I.E. was in the form of an annual grant to the University of Rs.1200/- i.e. Rs.100/- a month from his estate. Of this amount Rs.1000/- is to be regarded as coming from himself and Rs.200/- from his son, Diwan Dr. Badri Nath, the Private Secretary to His Highness of Kashmir. The announcement of the gift of Diwan Amar Nath was also received enthusiastically as the gathering realized that it really meant in capital value a gift of about Rs.30,000/- at 3.5 percent per annum.

The gifts of the three ministers – the Home Minister, Rai Bahadur Dr. A. Mitra, the Judicial Minister, Rai Bahadur Pandit Radha Kishen Kaul and the Revenue Minister, Sheikh Makbul Hussain amounted to Rs.500/- each.

While the other donations announced on the spot were as follows :-

1. Lala Shiv Das, Chief judge, Kashmir   Rs. 250/-
2. Choudhri Khushi Mohammad,   Rs.100/-
Governor Kashmir
3. General Bhag Singh, Officer Commanding,   Rs. 100/-
Kashmir Division
4. R.B. Col. Diwan Bishen Das   Rs. 250/-

5.	Bhai Dan Singh, Secretary to Chief Minister	Rs. 200/-
6.	Pandit Udey Chand, Secretary to H.H.	Rs. 200/-
7.	Col. Samandar Khan, Adjutant General	Rs. 50/-
8.	Col. Anant Ram, Quarter Master General	Rs. 100/-
9.	Maulvi Nazir Ahmed, Judge Small Cause Court	Rs. 20/-
10.	Pandit Parduman Kishen, Sub-Judge 1st Grade	Rs. 100/-
11.	R.S. Saradar Ganga Singh, D. En. Kashmir	Rs. 200/-
12.	Pandit J.C. Chatterji, Director Archaeology	Rs. 100/-
13.	L. Jagat Ram, Asstt. Secretary to C.M.	Rs. 50/-
14.	Bakshi Saradar Singh, Offg. Vernacular Secretary to H.H.	Rs. 25/-
15.	Mr. R.D. Pande, Secretary to Education Minister	Rs. 100/-
16.	Wazir Sobha Ram, General Treasurer	Rs. 500/-
17.	Saradar Mul Singh Khosla, P.A. to H.H.	Rs. 25/-
18.	L. Shanker Lal, P.A. to Home Minister	Rs. 50/-
19.	Malik Sher Mohammed, P.A. to R.M.	Rs. 15/-
20.	Diwan Bansi Lal P.A. to Settlement Commissioner	Rs. 50/-
21.	Pandit Suraj Ram Mattu, Treasury Officer	Rs. 50/-
22.	R.S.L. Govind, Offg. Astt. Accountant	Rs. 100/-
23.	L. Dyal Chand, Chief Supdt. Accountant General's Office	Rs. 75/-
24.	Pandit Daulat Ram, Examiner Local Accounts	Rs. 50/-
25.	Lala Ram Sarn, Inspector Police	Rs. 15/-
26.	L. Lal Chand, Deputy Inspector Police	Rs. 10/-
27.	Mehta Kripa Ram, tutor to the Maharajakumar	Rs. 10/-
28.	Diwan Brij Lal, Tahsildar, Srinagar	Rs. 25/-
29.	Bawa Balvant Singh, Inspector of Schools	Rs. 25/-
30.	Pandit Anant Ram, Supdt. Toshakhana	Rs. 50/-
31.	Pandit Kripa Ram, Supdt. Dharmarth	Rs. 50/-
32.	Wazir Pars Ram, Supdt. Police, Kashmir	Rs. 200/-
33.	Wazir Din Dayal, Tahvilsar Toshakhana	Rs. 100/-
34.	Pandit Deo Kak, Munsiff	Rs. 50/-
35.	Lala Sukh Dayal Sawhney, Sub. Judge	Rs. 50/-

2nd Grade

36. Pandit Kishen Lal, Munsiff	Rs. 25/-
37. Diwan Anant Ram Aswal, B.A., L.L.B	Rs. 100/-
38. Diwan Sahib Saran	Rs. 500/-
39. Pandit Vish Ram, Mgr Kashmir State property Bhadarwah Jagir	Rs. 100/-
40. Mr. L.C. Bose, Electrical engineer	Rs. 50/-
41. L. Niranjan Das, Head Master, State High School	Rs. 20/-
42. L. Shiv Chand, M.A. Professor Hindu College	Rs. 51/-
43. Pandit Gyani Ram, B.A.	Rs. 51/-
44. Lala Purshottam Ram, Hazirbash	Rs. 50/-
45. Col. Ishri Singh, Asstt. Adjutant General	Rs. 25/-
46. Major Bharat Singh	Rs. 15/-
47. Major Diwan Chet Ram, Deputy Asstt. Quarter Master General	Rs. 15/-
48. Major Isher Das, Supdt. C-in-C's office	Rs. 25/-
49. Saradar Gopal Singh S.D.O	Rs. 25/-
50. Lala Anant Sarup c/o of late Jora Mal	Rs. 51/-
51. Hakim Syed Hussain W.W. Ushampur	Rs. 25/-
52. Quarter Master General's Office, Cash	Rs. 25 /-
53. Babu Hari Chand, Photo Office	Rs. 15/-
54. Pandit Kashi Ram, Supdt. Foreign Office	Rs. 15/-
55. Pandit Inder Kishen, Accountant General's Office	Rs. 25/-
56. L. Sarni Mal, member Sanatan Dharma Sabha Kashmir	Rs. 25/-
57. L. Tara Chand Hakim Chief Minister and his son	Rs. 25/-
58. Bakshi Gokal Chand, Governor's Office	Rs. 15/-
59. Lala Balmukund, Accountant General's Office	Rs. 10/-
60. Pandit Rajkishen, Sub-Overseer	Rs. 10/-
61. Pandit Karm Chand, Agricultural Supdt.	Rs. 5/-
62. Pandit Tara Chand, Tahsildar Uri Cash	Rs. 15/-
63. Ram Lubhaya, Supdt. Revenue Minister's Office	Rs. 15/-

64. Pandit Sahib Mahadeo Rai, Cash	Re. 1/-
65. Four Friends	Rs. 30/-
66. Khwaja Samadju Kakru	Rs. 100/-
67. Saradar Ganga Singh, Mharajganj	Rs. 125/-
68. Pandit Vidh Lal Dhar, Rais of Kashmir	Rs. 250/-
69. Rai Gobind Ram's son	Rs. 15/-
70. Messers N.D. Hari Ram & Brothers	Rs. 500/-
71. Pandit Bisheshar Nath Razdan	Rs. 50/-
72. Saradar Hakim Singh Contractor	Rs. 500/-
73. Pandit Rishib Ram Contractor	Rs. 500/-
74. Pandit Isherjoo	Rs. 25/-
75. Thakur Ramchand of Peshawar	Rs. 100/-
76. Rai Bahadur Ram Saran Das, Rais of Lahore	Rs. 1000/-
77. Mir Waiz, Kashmir	Rs. 25/-
78. Akbar Shah	Rs. 12/-
79. Mian Wali Shah	Rs.5/-
80. Khwaja Hussan Shah	Rs. 6/-
81. Pandit Hargopal Vakil	Rs. 20/-
82. Mesers Jawahir Lal and Sons	Rs. 125/-
83. Pandit Salig Ram, Pleader, Cash	Rs. 10/-
84. Bakshi Moti Ram,	Rs. 25/-
85. L. Malawa Ram, Supdt. Agricultural Dept.	Rs. 10/-
86. Babu Isher Das, Supdt. Judge High Court's Office	Rs. 25/-
87. Pandit Vish Nath Photographer	Rs. 50/-
88. Pandit Din Dayal	Rs. 200/-
89. R.B. Girdhari Lal Mir Munshi to H.H. the Lt. Governor of Punjab	Rs. 100/-
90. Lala Shanker Das Isher Das, Maharajganj	Rs. 25/-
91. Dr. Din Dayal Das, Asstt. Surgeon Maharajganj	Rs. 25/-
92. Lala Tara Chand incharge Director Agriculture	Rs. 15/-
93. L. Ram Kishen Newspaper Reader to His Highness	Rs. 10/-
94. Lala Devi Dayal Lodi Ram, Maharajganj	Rs. 10/-
95. Lala Radhakishen Mohan Singh	Rs. 15/-
96. Lala Sobha Ram Shaker Das	Rs. 10/-

97. Pandit Hari Ram	Rs. 15/-
98. Maharaja Sahib's cricket team	Rs. 25/-
99. Pandit Autar Kishen Professor Hindu College	Rs. 51/-
100. Sultan Mutwali KhaJagirdar Kathai	Rs. 250/-
101.Babu Charanjit Lala Manager Bharat Bank Srinagar	Rs. 10/-
102. Mr. C.J. Burrow, State Band Master	Rs. 10/-
103. Pandit Sona Dar, Vakil	Rs. 20/-
104. Thakur Raghunath Singh, Asstt. Supdt. Stables	Rs. 10/-
105. Pandit Nityanand Shastri	Rs. 5/-
106. Lala Karam Chand of Emnabad	Rs. 10/-
107.Pandit Jia Lal Dar	Rs. 50/-
108. Bhagat Khazana Mal Goor Das, Maharajganj	Rs. 50/-
109. Sukh Dayal Amar Chand	Rs. 50/-
110.Lala Fateh Chand Deputy Inspector Customs & Excise	Rs. 10/-
111.Seth Phattu (H.H.'s Private Deptt.)	Rs. 200/-
112. Thakur Raghunath Singh	Rs. 25/-
113.Pandit Mani Ram	Rs.15/-
114.Pandit Tara Mani Cash	Rs. 50/-
115.Lala Ram Singh	Rs. 15/-
116.Lala Shiv Nath	Rs. 25/-
117. Pandit Vishva Nath Pujari	Rs. 50/-
118.L.N. Sharma	Rs. 120/-

With these announcements ... two committees were formed – one for Srinagar and the other for Jammu for the collection of the promised donations and subscriptions and for getting new ones.

Throughout the meeting great enthusiasm prevailed which it was most elevating to behold. By the time the proceedings came to an end it had already grown dark and lamps had to be lighted when at about 9 p.m. the meeting dispersed with a vote of thanks to the chair and cheers for the King Emperor, for His Highness the President and for the Maharaja Bahadur of Darbhanga."

The above mentioned Report throws much light on how successfully the Kashmir Deputation worked. Besides the large number of Hindu donors, there were also Muslims who contributed to the Hindu University fund as much as they could efford. The Report includes the names of even those who promised to pay quite meager amount. However, it is important to note that that their contributions were also recognized. Soon, on 28 July, 1912, a meeting of Pradhan Bhumihar Brahman Sabha was held at Bankipur to felicitate the Darbhanga for his achievements and his efforts for the Hindu University[20]. It indicates his popularity and commitment to the cause of the Hindu University.

A few months later, Darbhanga mentioned the details of his programme for the tour of the delegation seeking donation for the Hindu University in his letter of 12 December, 1912, to Butler. He wrote[21]:

> "… my personal idea is to go to Mirzapur on 4 January then to Allahabad, Jhansi, Gwalior, Jaipur, Jodhpur, Bikaner, Patiala and to the Punjab … then go to Delhi and take instructions from you before going to Bombay and Kathyawar. The difficulty about Southern India is that I can not get any one who would undertake to clear the ground and arrange meetings before I go."

Malaviya also wrote a letter (24 December, 1912) to Butler saying that Gaekwar had granted him interview, but had not made any commitment regarding his donation. He, it seems, also depended on Butler and requested him to mobilize Gaekwar in this context[22]. The text of the letter is given below:

> "H.H. the Gaekwar was pleased to grant me an interview yesterday. I explained to him how we propose to proceed in the matter of religious education. … he was glad to see that I had progressed towards liberalism, and seemed on the whole to be favourably disposed towards the Scheme. He said however that he wanted further time to consider the matter and has asked me to see him at Baroda. But my anxiety for

the accomplishment of the scheme yet makes me desire and pray that His Highness might be pleased to announce his donation at an early date."

Darbhanga, however, began to communicate with Jodhpur, Jaipur, Bhabnagar, Kapurthala and others for the visit of his deputation[23]. Sundaram[24] writes in this context that the Deputation (of Darbhanga, the President, accompanied with Malaviya, Sundar Lal and others) visited Allahabad (on 21 January, 1913), Nabha, Bikanir (on 1 February, 1913) Jodhpur (on 3 February, 1913), Udaipur (on 15 February, 1913), Indore (on 18 February, 1913), and Bombay (on 23 February, 1913). At all these places, response was very positive and encouraging.

On 28 April, 1913, Darbhanga sent a long report to Butler on the basis of the information received from Sundar Lal regarding the financial position of the Society. Further, he also requested him (Butler) to suggest the steps to be taken "to bring into existence the Hindu University at an early date". The text of this report is given below[25]:

"Dated Darbhanga, the 28th April 1913

From: The Hon'ble Maharaj Sir Rameshwar Singh Bahadur, K.C.I.E., of Darbhanga, Bankipur

To: The Hon'ble Sir Harcourt Butler, K.C.I.E., C.I.E.

I have much pleasure in addressing you on the subject of the Hindu University. I have now obtained detailed information as to ... financial position from Rai Bahadur Pandit Sundar Lal.

2. I propose, in the first place, to explain our exact financial position and, in the second place, to suggest for your consideration and advice the steps that we might now take to bring into existence the Hindu University at an early date.

3. As to the financial position, as you are already aware, the subscriptions promised go well over 80 lakhs. We have not yet gone to the great bulk of the Native States throughout India. We have approached only a few of them, and have received liberal responses. I hope in the next winter to pay a visit to Mysore and Southern India. The amount, however, actually received from the subscribers up to date is Rs. 21,37. 539-8-11.5. Out of this sum the amount in the hands of the Society directly is Rs. 21, 08, 180-2-5.5. The balance of Rs.2,359-6-6 is In the hands of the Secretaries of local committees or private Banks or persons who have been carrying on the work of collections. The amount of course will be coming into the Allahabad office in the ordinary course. The amount collected has been mainly invested in Government Promissory Notes. We own today Government Promissory Notes of the face value of Rs. 21,59,000, carrying interest at 3.5 percent, and the uninvested amount is being invested in the same way. The capital fund in hand may thus be roughly said to be Rs. 20,80,769-4-6 invested in purchasing Government Promissory Notes and Rs. 84,189-1-2.5 in other forms; total Rs. 21,64, 958-5-8.5, including interest (Rs.25,063-11-6) and miscellaneous receipts (Rs. 2,355-1-3).

4. Besides this amount the following amounts which have been granted by the Ruling Chiefs have yet to be collected:-

1. His Highness the Maharaja of Gwalior Rs.5 lakhs
2. ditto Alwar   Rs. 2 lakhs
3. ditto Bikanir   Rs. 1 lakh
4. ditto Nabha   Rs. 1 lakh
5. ditto Benaras   Rs. 1 lakh
6. ditto Jodhpur   Rs. 1 lakh   -----------------
                              Total   Rs. 11 lakhs

5. In addition to this there is a sum of Rs. 3 lakhs on account of the balance of my donation. These may be taken almost as paid, as they will be realized as soon as the Government desires that the amounts should be paid in. These amounts total 14 lakhs.

6. In addition to these amounts the Maharaja of Cossimbazar is transferring property in trust of the value of one lakh which would bring Rs.3,500 a year and Babu Brajendra Kishore Roy Chaudhry, who

is also a donor of one lakh, is similarly transferring property which would bring us Rs.3,500 a year more net. In other words, they will not pay the money in cash but propose to give property which will bring an equal amount of net income. I am expecting drafts of the necessary documents from these gentlemen.

7. Besides these I may mention the names of the following donors of Rs.50,000 and above, whose donations I expect there will be no difficulty whatsoever in collecting:-

1. Raja Kalanand Singh and the Hon'ble   Rs. 1 Lakh
   Kuwar Krityanand Singh of Raj Banaily
2. The Maharani of Hathwa   Rs. 1 Lakh
3. The Hon'ble Rana Sir Sheo Raj Singh   Rs. 1.25 lakh
   of Khajurgaon, Raibareli
4. Seth Narotem Maraji Gokul Das   Rs. 1 Lakh
   (ex-Sheriff of Bombay)
5. Thakur Suraj Bux Singh, Taluqdar   Rs. 65,000
   of Kasmanda, Sitapur
   (out of 1 lakh 35000 having been paid)
6. Raja Kristo Das Law   Rs. 75,000
7. Rai Ram Charan Das Bahadur   Rs. 75,000
8. Balance still payable out of Rai   Rs. 25,000   Bahadur   Sundar
   Lal's donation of one lakh)   _____ Total   Rs. 6,65,000

8. There are of course a very large number of donors of amounts below Rs.50,000. Thus in Allahabad alone may be mentioned the names of:-

    1. Lala Bisheshar Das   Rs. 25,000
    2. Choudhry Mahadeo Prasad   Rs. 25,000
    3. Raja Sahib of Manda   Rs. 20,000
    4. Lala Shambhu nath   Rs. 20,000
     Lachhmi Narain

In Lucknow, Rai Prag Narain Bhargava Bahadur has paid Rs. 5,000 out of his donation of Rs. 30,000. His balance of Rs.25,000 will be paid up in a few days. Raja Ram Pal Singh, who is a donor of Rs. 20,000 has paid Rs. 10,000. The balance of Rs. 10,000 will be paid later on. I need not take into account the vast number of donors of smaller amounts who have paid in part their donations, and from most of whom there will be no difficulty in recovering the balance.

9. Three Ruling Chiefs have granted in perpetuity the payment of the following sums:-

His Highness the Maharaja of Jodhpur	Rs.24,000
His Highness the Maharaja of Kashmir	Rs. 12,000
His Highness the Maharaja of Bikanir	Rs. 12,000
	————
Total	Rs. 48,000

These allowances when capitalized at the rate of 3.5 percent come to about 14 lakhs in value. There are other persons besides who have promised annual or monthly donations in various amounts.

10. Taking the amounts shown in paragraphs 2 to 8 of this letter the amount of the money in hand which may be safely taken as already in hand may be set forth as below:-

(a) Net amount already in hand,   Rs. 21,38,738
including interest realized

(b) Amount to be paid by Ruling   Rs. 14,00,000
Chiefs and the Hon'ble the
Maharaja of Darbhanga

(c) Amount which will be paid in   Rs. 2,00,000
property as per paragraph 5

(d) Amount of donations above   Rs. 6,65,000
Rs. 50,000 as per paragraph 6

(e) Capitalised value of annual   Rs. 14,00,000
grants by the Ruling Chiefs
As per paragraph 8   ------------------

           Total   Rs. 58,03,738

11. The great bulk of the balance I have not taken into account for the purpose of this note, although it includes items like Rs. 10,000 each granted by the two Maharanis of Bikaner and Rs. 5,000 of the Maharaj Kumar, Rs. 5,000 by Raj Kumar Hari Singh Saheb of Jammu and Kashmir, Rs. 1,200 per annum by Rai Saheb Dewan

Amar Nath, C.I.E., of Kashmir, Rs. 25,000 by Dewan Daya Kishen Kaul of Alwar, Rs. 10,000 by Pandit Sukhdeo Prasad C.I.E., retired Minister, Marwar State, Rs. 50,000 of Raj Kumar Harihar Prasad of Amawan, Rs. 20,000 of Babu Kamta Shiromani Prasad Singh, Taluqdar of Sehipur, Fyzabad, Rs. 15,000 of Thakurain Sriram Koer, Taluqdar of Khapradih and Rs. 5,000 of Srimati Jank Bai of Bithoor, all in landed property; Rs. 15,000 of Thakur Ganga Bux Singh of Tikari, Rai Bareili, balance of Rs. 15,000 of Raja Chandra Shekhar of Sissendy and Rs. 10,000 of Raja Lalta Prasad of Pilibhit, Rs.15,000 each of Raja Udai Raj Singh of Kashipur and the Hon'ble Raja Kushal Pal Singh of Kotla.

12 We have not taken into consideration the value of the Central Hindu College which if I remember aright the Hon'ble Mr. Sharp put down at about Rs. 14 lakhs. The amount which the Hon'ble Mr. Sharp thought will be required was between Rs. 40 lakhs and Rs. 50 lakhs. I think, taking into consideration the amount mentioned in paragraph 9, which may be taken to be as realized for all practical purposes, we have raised more than the amount required, and I think we are now in a position to ask the Government to be so good as to take into consideration the legislation necessary for bringing the University into existence. We have thus financially made out a good case, and if the work proceed as it has been going on till now we shall be able to collect a much larger amount.

You are pleased to communicate to the Hon'ble the Raja of Mahmudabad intimation of the fact that the Government had granted one lakh a year recurring to the Muslim University. This was in addition to the large amount that the Government was already paying to the M.A.O. College, Aligarh, and which of course would be continued on its incorporation with the Muslim University. The cost of the necessary buildings and apparatus for the fitting up of a first class University is very heavy. The figures recently prepared for the Dacca University Scheme give an idea of the amount required. It is now evident by the reason of the curtailment of the scope of the University we cannot get any large amount from Bengal or the Punjab, nor from Madras or Bombay. The Central Provinces as well as the new province of Bihar and Orissa are each looking forward to the establishment of their own Provincial Universities. Our situation has thus become more difficult by reason of the curtailment of the scope of our own Hindu University as well as by reason of the expected establishment of other Universities. I think that the Government of India in view of the above circumstances should be able to see its way to giving us a much larger recurring grant, as also a substantial non-recurring grant for buildings, etc. I do not know at what figure we can put our expectations; but three lakhs a year would perhaps be not thought too much to suggest, and a moiety of the cost of buildings, etc. You can best advise us how to approach the Government in this matter. The University is of course to be a residential one, and the cost of the construction of the necessary hostel and their maintenance and up keep have also to be taken into consideration.

14 Turning now to the other question, I think that the new University should have if possible the following faculties, viz.
1. Oriental
2. Theological
3. Arts
4. Science (pure and applied).
5. Law.

The Oriental Faculty, the main object of which will be to foster the study of Sanskrit and its literature, etc., will appeal very largely to the public. My idea is that the studies in that Faculty should be directed by a European Sanskrit scholar of standing and experience, assisted by some Indian Professors who should also be scholars of English. In addition to them we shall require a large staff of Pandits of the old class. We should endeavour to collect famous Pandits in every department of Sanskrit learning who are to be found in various parts of India.

Benares is the sacred place of the Hindus to which every pious member of that community aspires to go in the evening of his life. I expect that a good number of eminent Pandits would be attracted to it if suitable honorarium or salary is fixed for their support and maintenance and we should soon collect at Kashi the best Pandits of India. Another object of the Oriental Faculty should be to collect and bring together all works now extant in Sanskrit, either in print or preserved in manuscripts. There are yet treasured up many valuable works in Native States and in the families of old Pandits to which the Hindu University can obtain access easily. In this work the Pandits will materially assist. The cultivation of the vernaculars would be another feature of the work of that faculty. I think we shall require about Rs. 6,000 a month to begin work on a suitable scale, and the amount will of course have to be increased as the work develops. A large number of Hindu students from all parts of India still come to Benares for study. They maintain themselves with the help of many charities and chhatras now existing in Benares. If the Hindu University open its doors to them we shall then have a class of students who undertake to study Sanskrit not with the object of seeking employment under the Government but for the sake of study itself. The nobility and gentry of India will continue to help the scholars in the manner in which they have been helped in the past and are now being helped. This should supplement the work of the University in its own special department.

15   The faculty of Arts and Science would for the present work on the lines of the faculties in these subjects in the existing Universities. The cost of these departments will depend upon the number of chairs which we can establish and the subjects of study that we propose to take up. There is a great demand for technical education in connection with the Hindu University. That however is a branch of instruction which can swallow up any amount of money. The Maharaja of Jodhpur has given Rs. 24,000 a year for a Professor in some technical subject, and I think it may be possible to inaugurate the study of some special branch of

technical education. This will come under the heading Applied Science for the present – to be expanded into a Faculty of Technology later on.

The faculty of law will be practically self-supporting. We will have to specialize in Hindu Law and its study from original sources.

16 The Hon'ble Rai Pandit Sunder Lal Bahadur in his letter to me says:-

"In the scheme which I outlined in a note prepared by me last year I indicated my views though necessarily on limited scale. The cost of running the University apart from its tuitional side was to be met from examination fees such as the existing Universities levy. I do not know whether the Government will be prepared to allow us to hold a Matriculation Examination in various centres and recognized schools as the existing Universities do. I should like vey much to know how far the Government will be inclined to accede to the suggestions made by us in our letter to the Hon'ble Sir Harcourt Butler, dated the 25th October 1912, which you submitted to Sir Harcourt Butler on behalf of the Society. If the Government in view of the financial position explained by me above considers that we have made out a sufficient case for asking for legislation in the ensuing cold weather, I will be very glad, as soon as the rains set in, to undertake to draft the Constitution of the University and its Statutes and Regulations and to shipshape them during the High Court vacation, for submission to the Government to form the basis of discussion. The fundamental points can be settled by personal discussion wherever necessary".

17 I shall be very glad to come and see you in Simla in the second week of May."

Sundaram also included this report (along with the names of donors) in his book[26]. It is clear that besides Bikanir, Gwalior and a few other ruling chiefs, the elites of Bihar, Bengal, and U.P. made substantial contribution. However, it may be noted that Malaviya's name does not figure anywhere on the list of donors. Mrs. Besant's contribution was considered to be highest (Rs.14 lakhs).

On 2 June, 1913, Butler wrote in reply to Darbhanga suggesting several points to be considered important by the Society. A copy of this letter is given below[27]:

"Demi-Official Letter no. 117-Edn., dated Simla, the 2nd June 1913

From – The Hon'ble Sir Harcourt Butler, K.C.I.E., C.I.E.

To – The Hon'ble Maharaja Sir Rameshwar Singh Bahadur, K.C.I.E. of Darbhanga.

I have to thank you for your letter of the 28th April 1913 in which you explain your exact financial position and suggest for my consideration and advice the steps that might now be taken to bring into existence the Hindu University at an early date.

I regret that I am not in a position to indicate the lines on which the Constitution of the University should be framed. The matter is still under consideration and reference to the Secretary of State is necessary. Nor am I in a position to make any statement as to finance. I would, however, point out that the figure of 50 lakhs attributed to Mr. Sharp was only a rough estimate of the capitalized value of the recurring expenditure probably required to conduct a University of a thousand students, and did not include capital expenditures. Also the Hindu College was valued at 27 not 14 lakhs. But I note your desire to go ahead with the preparation of a scheme and it will perhaps be of some assistance to you to know the conditions the fulfillment of which the Government of India regard as precedent to the introduction of any scheme. These are:-

(i) That a suitable site be provided;

(ii) That the Central Hindu College be transferred to the University;

(iii) That a sum of 50 lakhs must be collected. In this amount may be included the capitalized value of the property mentioned in paragraph 6 of your letter and the perpetual grants mentioned in paragraph 9 of your letter, provided the documentary title is satisfactory in the case of the latter and possession of the property has been made over in the case of the former;

(iv) That the Constitution of the University (should) proceed on lines to be indicated to you hereafter;

(v) That a committee appointed for the purpose (should) report that the Central Hindu College is fit to be developed into a residential and teaching University.

Should progress be as satisfactory as you consider that you have reason to hope, I shall be very glad to meet the Hon'ble Rai Pandit Sundar Lal Bahadur during the High Court vacation. The Secretary of State, as you are aware, has reserved full discretion in regard to every detail of any scheme that may eventually be laid before him."

Darbhanga, then, continued to persuade Butler for mobilizing Jaipur and Gwalior to support the Hindu University movement and give donation to its fund[28]. In the context of the progress made so far by the Society for the Hindu University the following Report was published in <u>London Times</u> of 27 June, 1913[29]:

27 June 1913
THE PROPOSED HINDU UNIVERSITY
London Times

*Correspondence which has recently passed between the **Maharaja of Darbhanga, who is at the head of the movement to create a Hindu University in India**, and Sir Harcourt Butler, the Education Member of the Governor-General's Council, has been published. The Maharaja, surveying the financial position,* *intimated that the subscriptions promised amounted to more than 80 lakhs of rupees (£533,333), of which about £140,000 had been received. Taking into account the capital value of certain grants of property and annual payments in perpetuity granted by three Ruling Chiefs, he estimated the amount which was in hand, or which might be safely taken as already in hand, to be not far short of £400,000, exclusive of the value of the Central Hindu College at Benares. He claimed that a good case had been made out financially for the Government to take into consideration the legislation necessary for bringing the University into being.*

Sir Harcourt Butler replied that the matter was still under consideration; but it would, perhaps, be of some assistance to the promoters to know the conditions which the Government of India regarded as precedent to the introduction of any scheme. These were the provision of a suitable site; the transfer of the Central Hindu College to the University; and the collection of not less than £333,333. In this amount might be included the capitalized value of the property mentioned by the Maharaja, and the perpetual grants by three Ruling Chiefs, provided that the documentary title was satisfactory in the case of the latter and the possession of the property had been made over in the case of the former. The further conditions were that the constitution of the University should proceed on lines to be indicated by the Government, and that a Committee be appointed to report whether the Central Hindu College was fit to be developed into a residential and teaching University. (emphasis added)

The report mentioned above is very clear and gives only two names, Darbhanga as the person heading the movement for the Hindu University at Banaras and Sir Harcourt Butler, the Education Member in the Council.

On 14 July, 1913, Sundar Lal, Hon. Secretary of the Society for Hindu University, sent a letter along with a report containing an account of income and expenditure of the Society[30]. The text of the letter is given below:

"The Hindu University Society
Registered Under Act XXI of 1860

No. 400 10

4. Couper Road
Allahabad
14ᵗʰ July, 1913

My dear Maharaja Saheb Bahadur,

As desired by you the capitalized value of the permanent annual grants of Bikaner, Kashmir and Jodhpur Darbars have been included in the daily report (copy enclosed) and will also be shown in the Statements to the press in future.

A Statement of our total receipts (including interest) in the Bank and as otherwise disposed of has been prepared as called for by you, and is herewith sent.

Yours sincerely
Sundar Lal

On 31 August, 1913, Maharaja of Alwar wrote in reply to Darbhanga's letter, of 23 August, 1913, showing his concern for the provision of affiliation of his schools in the proposed University and suggested him to give probable dates for his Deputation's visit to Alwar. The text of his letter is given below[31]:

'*My dear Maharaja Sahib,*

Many thanks for your Highness' letter of the 23ʳᵈ instant.

Regarding the affiliation of our schools to the Hindu University, I am thinking of talking this matter over personally with His Excellency the Viceroy as well as with the Education Member when I happen to see them at Delhi or Simla.

So far as I can say at present I think I shall probably be in my capital from December to February, but it is very difficult to make out a fixed programme so far ahead. If your Highness, however, could give probable dates that would suit you to visit Alwar, I shall perhaps be in a position to inform you where I may be likely to be on those dates.

With kind regards,
Yours sincerely,
Jay Singh"

Regarding Alwar's concern for his schools, Malaviya wrote the following to Butler on 25 September, 1913[32]:

"I hear that H.H. the Maharaja of Alwar has come to Simla. If so, he will of course see you as he told me when I went to see him at Alwar last month, that he wished to speak to you about the question of the recognition of schools by the Hindu University. I hope you will kindly set his mind at rest on the question and advise him to pay up the amount he has promised..."

It seems that Malaviya had visited Alwar sometime before Alwar wrote his letter to Darbhanga (mentioned above) on 31 August, 1913. However, Malaviya's letter indicates that his visit could not be effective for securing Alwar's contribution.

On 10 October, 1913, Darbhanga wrote the following to Butler[33]:

"I hear that His Highness the Maharaja of Gwalior has intimated to you his willingness to put the five lakhs whenever you desire it to be paid. I shall feel very much obliged if you will let me know whether this information is correct as it will greatly facilitate the task of collection(of) the remaining amount we have got to collect.

Have you received the expected despatch from the Secretary of State? Will you kindly let me know whether You will be in Simla in January and February."

A meeting of the Committee of Management of the Hindu University Society was held on 30 October, 1913. The details of the proceedings are given below[34]:

The Hindu University Society

'*Proceedings of an adjourned meeting of the Committee of Management of the Hindu University Society held at 9, Elgin Road, Allahabad, on the 30th October, 1913 at 3 p.m.*

Present:

Mahamahopadhyaya Pundit Aditya Ram Bhattacharya, M.A.

The Hon'ble Pandit Madan Mohan Malaviya, B. A., Ll.D.

Dr. Satish Chandra Banerji, M.A., Ll.D.

The Hon'ble Dr. Tej Bahadur Sapru, M.A.Ll.D

Babu Ishwar Saran, B.A.

Babu Bhagwan Das, M.A.

Babu Gauri Shankar Prasad, B.A., Ll.B

Prof. Benoy Kumar Sarkar, M.A.

Pandit Baldev Ram Dave

The Hon'ble Dr. Sundar Lal, C.I.E., Ll.D.
1. *Dr. Satish Chandra Banerji was unanimously voted to the Chair.*
2. *In connection with the question of the incorporation of the Central Hindu College, Benares, the resolutions of that body as well as the previous resolutions of the Committee of Management of the Hindu*

University Society and the letter of Sir Harcourt Butler, dated the 2ⁿᵈ June 1913, were read and considered.

Resolved that the Central Hindu College, Benaras, be incorporated with the Hindu University Society subject to the following conditions, viz.:-

1. *That all the funds, properties, moveable and immoveable, and all assets held by the said Association as its property, or in trust, and dues belonging to, or owned by it, do vest in, and be transferred to, the Hindu University Society, except the funds expressly endowed for the maintenance of the Central Hindu College Girls' School, as to which the question will be considered at the next meeting of the Committee.*

2. *That the Hindu University Society keep up and maintain the present Central Hindu College with the Ranavir Pathshala and the Central Hindu Collegiate Schools to serve as the nucleus of the Hindu University proposed to be established.*

3. *That for the said purpose the Hindu University Society appoint such Committee or Committees as it may think fit and proper, and define and regulate the powers and the constitution of the said Committee or Committees, and from time to time amend or modify the same.*

4. *That the present Trustees of the Central Hindu College be appointed members of the Hindu University Society under Rule 3(d) of the Rules of this Society, it being always understood that such appointment does not necessitate or require their nomination, or the nomination of any of them, to the membership of the Governing Body of the Hindu University when it is established.*

5. *That the Hindu University Society make such provision as it may think proper from time to time or the maintenance of the said institutions out of the funds which shall vest in it by reason of the incorporation of the Central Hindu College with it, and to allot at its discretion any further funds it may think proper for the said purpose*

6. *That on the establishment of the Hindu University, the Hindu University Society shall set apart such portion of the funds so transferred to the Hindu University Society from the Central Hindu College as the Hindu University Society may consider proper for the maintenance of the School*

and shall arrange for its working and governance in such manner as it may consider fit and proper.

3. *Resolved that the above Resolution be laid before the Annual General Meeting of the Society to be held on the 2nd December, 1913 and that in the meanwhile it may be communicated to the Secretary, Board of Trustees, Central Hindu College, Benares.*

4. *Resolved that a sub-committee consisting of the Hon'ble Dr. Sundar Lal, Dr. Satish Chandra Banerji, the Hon'ble Dr. Tej Bahdur Sapru and Babu Iswar Saran be formed to submit proposals for carrying out the above Resolution and to formulate a Scheme for the proper working of the Central Hindu College, the Ranavir Pathshala and the Collegiate School, and the trustees of the Central Hindu College be requested to nominate three representatives to co-operate with them in preparing the same.*

5. *Resolved that the above Sub-Committee be also requested to consider and report as to the desirability and feasibility of the Hindu University taking up the management of the Girl's School and its funds and properties. The Sub-Committee to report before the 2nd December, 1913.*

6. *In connection with Resolution No.4 of this meeting held on the 26ᵗʰ October, 1913 the Honorary Secretary suggested that the following principle might be adopted in selecting Banks with which arrangements might be made for the receipt and transmission of donations from outstations.*

(1) That the Bank or Banks selected should have an office or branch at Allahabad, Benaras or Lucknow.

(2) That the Banks should agree to transmit the monies paid in to them or their branches free of charge to Allahabad as promptly as possible.

(3) That notice of payments made by district committees or donors be regularly sent to this Office as soon as practicable after such payment and that the Government Promissory Notes which may be ordered to be purchased and forwarded to this office at a rate not exceeding 0-2-0 percent.

(4) That the District Committees and donors be requested to deal as far as possible with the Bank of Bengal or its branch if there be one in in their district; and to transmit monies as early as convenient to Allahabad.

The suggestions were approved and adopted and were to be given effect to in revising the list of Banks.

With a vote of thanks to the Chair the meeting dispersed.

Sundar Lal   Satish Chandra Banerji
Honorary Secretary   Chairman"

The above mentioned meeting of the Committee of Management of the Hindu University Society, it seems, following the agreement (dated the 22nd October, 1911, mentioned before) between Darbhanga, Malaviya and Mrs. Besant, deals mainly with the methods and procedures to be adopted for the amalgamation of the Central Hindu College with the Hindu University. On 6 November, 1913, Alwar informed Darbhanga that he was satisfied by the Viceroy and Butler regarding the Hindu University project. Further, he wrote that other related issues would also be satisfactorily settled[35]. On 10 December, 1913, Sundar Lal, Hon. Secretary of the Hindu University Society, wrote to Darbhanga about his being re-elected as the President of the Society unanimously. The text of this letter is given below[36]:

The Hindu University Society
Registered Under Act XXI of 1860

4, Couper Road No. 1220
Allahabad
10 December, 1913

The Hon'ble Maharaja Sir Rameshwara Singh Bahadur, K.C.I.E., Darbhanga

My dear Sir,
I am glad to inform you that at the Second Annual General Meeting of this Society held on the 7th instant you were unanimously reelected as President of the Committee of Management of the Society for the ensuing year.(emphasis added)

Yours sincerely
Sundar Lal
Honorary Secretary

It may be noted here that there were eminent lawyers (such as Tej Bahadur Sapru, Seshagiri Iyer, Krishna Sahay and others) great intellectuals (such as Profesor Radha Kumud Mukherji, Professor Benoy Kumar Sarkar, Mm. Aditya Ram Bhattacharya, Bhagawan Das and others) besides famous zamindars and elites of the country on the Committee of Management of the Hindu University Society. Mere status of Darbhanga as a great zamindar could hardly have been effective for influencing them to take a unanimous decision. Probably, it was his commitment to the cause of the University, his tact of mobilizing higher authorities of the Government in favour of the Hindu University project, and, his zeal and the painstaking effort displayed in the course of visiting different corners of the country, which impressed the members (of the Society) so much that they reelected him (Darbhanga) unanimously as the President of the Committee of Management.

On 11 December, 1913, Darbhanga wrote to Butler about his inability to write to him for a long time due to his illness. He mentioned that[37]:

"A long protracted illness of several weeks duration has precluded me from writing to you for some time.

The Viceroy told me to come to Delhi after the Secretary of State's despatch is received. As there was little prospect of this before the end of February and as March is a very busy month for the Government. I am afraid, I shall not have to come before April. Will you kindly let me know when you leave Delhi and when you arrive at Simla."

A few weeks later, on 6 January, 1914, Malaviya wrote to Butler the following letter[38]:

"Maharaja Balrampur has promised to decide after returning to Balrampur, what sum he will contribute to the Hindu University Fund. I had asked him for five lakhs, but finding him unwilling to give that sum, I have suggested that he should give at least three lakhs, so that a Balrampur Chair may be established to commemorate hin generosity. I hope that you will kindly say a word to him. We shall then be sure to get a handsome amount".
(emphasis added)

It will not be out of place to note here that Malaviya seems to have altogether ignored Darbhanga and instead of bringing Balrampur experience (of his failure) to the notice of the President (Darbhanga) of the Society, approached Butler directly for his help. No evidence of Butler's reply (to his letter) has been available so far. Since Malaviya was considered to be a man of questionable conduct by the top authorities of the Government then[39], Butler might have decided to ignore him. His (Malaviya's) earlier request to Butler, bypassing Darbhanga, for mobilizing Alwar (mentioned before) had also not been acknowledged by him (Butler).

On 23 December 1912 attempt was made to assassinate Lord Hardinge. The political situation following this incident remained disturbed for a few months. Then, Darbhanga wrote to Sir Harcourt Butler on 19 January, 1914, expressing his deep concern for the health of the Viceroy and condemning the attack. He requested Butler to communicate his personal message to the Viceroy that he was pleased to know that the Viceroy was recovering fast and would soon be able to shoulder the burden of the administration. He, further, wrote that[40],

> *"I need not dilate upon what we owe you – we are fully aware that but for you and the Viceroy the Scheme would have been long ago consigned to the waste paper basket and I will tell my people when I meet them at Allahabad that they may place their implicit reliance and repose their entire confidence in the friend that has in the past and will, I am perfectly sure, ever stand with them in the future."*

Subsequently, on July 18, 1914, Butler sent a letter to Darbhanga giving a wide range of guideline in respect of the Constitution, powers, etc., of the proposed University. Pioneer of Allahabad also reported the entire letter on 24 July, 1914. The text of this letter is given below[41]:

"Demi-Official No. 202- Education
Simla, the 18th July, 1914.
My dear Maharaja Bahadur,

Please refer to my letter to you, No.117- Education, dated Simla, the 2nd June, 1913, in which I regretted that I was not yet in a position to indicate the lines on which the constitution of the University should be framed, as the matter was still under consideration and reference to His Majesty's Secretary of the State was necessary, but noted your desire to go ahead with the preparation of a scheme and thought it would be of assistance to you to know the conditions the fulfillment of which the Government of India regarded as necessarily precedent to the introduction of any scheme. These were:-

"(i) That a suitable site be provided;

(ii) That the Central Hindu College be transferred to the University;

(iii) That a sum of Rs.50 lakhs must be collected. In this amount may be included the capitalised value of the property mentioned in paragraph 6 of your letter and the perpetual grants mentioned in paragraph 9 of your letter, provided the documentary title is satisfactory in the case of the latter and possession of the property has been made over in the case of the former.

(iv) That the constitution of the University proceed on lines to be indicated to you hereafter;

(i) That a committee appointed for the purpose report that the Central Hindu College is fit to be developed into a residential and teaching University."

2. I understand that substantial progress has been made in regard to (i), (ii) and (iii), and action can at any time be taken under (v).

    As regards (iv), I am now in a position to make a further important communication to you.

3. It has been an understanding throughout that in essentials and especially in regard to their relations to Government the proposed Hindu and Muhammadan Universities should be on the same footing. As you are aware, the Muhammadan University Committee have not accepted the constitution laid down in the case of the proposed Muhammadan University at Aligarh. As regards the relations of the proposed University to Government, the original proposal of the Muhammadan University Committee was that the Viceroy should be Chancellor with powers of intervention and control. It was decided, and finally decided, that this should not be. The scheme offered to the University Committee left the University, through the Court, power to appoint their own Chancellor while it gave the Governor-General in Council the necessary powers of intervention and control. This arrangement was considerably criticized at the time. In consequence the Government of India and His Majesty's Secretary of State have reconsidered the whole question with every desire to assist a solution. They recognize that the Government of India is an impersonal body situated at a distance and cannot give that close personal attention to the University which is required in the case of a new institution of a novel type in India. On a review of all the circumstances of the case, and the criticisms which have been advanced, the Government of India

and His Majesty's Secretary of State have come to the conclusion that the best form of constitution will be to constitute the Lieutenant Governor of the United Provinces ex-officio Chancellor of the University with certain opportunities for giving advice and certain powers of intervention and control. The Hindu University, though not empowered to affiliate colleges from outside, will be Imperial in the sense that, subject to regulations, it will admit students from all parts of India. On the other hand, it will be localized in or by Benares. There will be obvious advantages in having as Chancellor of the University the Lieutenant-Governor of the Province, who is also Chancellor of the Allahabad University, and who will be able to help to correlate the work between the two, to secure them corresponding advantages, and to foster a spirit of healthy co-operation. Moreover, such a constitution is in accord with the general policy of decentralization which is now pursued by the Government of India.

4. *As regards the powers which it is necessary to reserve to the Chancellor, these are:-*

(a) *The right of general supervision and power to advice that such action be taken and such staff be appointed or removed as will secure the objects of the University, with power, if necessary, to see that such advice be given effect to.*

(b) *The right of inspection for purpose of seeing whether the standard of education is kept up sufficiently high and for other purposes.*

(c) *The right, as a special measure, to appoint, if necessary (as the result of such inspection or otherwise), examiners for the University examinations, who would report to the Chancellor.*

(d) *The annual receipt of accounts.*

(e) *The approval of the appointments of Vice-Chancellor and Provost.*

(f) *The approval of initial regulations, etc., and of subsequent changes.*

(g) *The approval of the incorporation of local colleges in the University.*

(h) *The nomination of the five members to the Senate; and*

(i) *The approval of the institution of new faculties and the reservation of power to lay down the limits of expansion at any particular time.*

Some of these powers have been suggested by your Committee. Others are emergency powers which may never be exercised and can be exercised only very occasionally. The principle underlying them all is that in the interest of the rising generation and the parents, the Government must be in co-operation with the University and in a position to help it effectively and secure sound finance. The interests of the Government and the students and their parents in this matter are necessarily identical.

As you are already aware, the decision in regard to affiliation of outside colleges is final. It was realized at the time that this decision would cause some disappointment; but I may take this opportunity to observe that it was not reached without due notices to the University Committees. At an informal meeting of the Constitution Committee of the Muhammadan University, held at Simla on the 23rd September, 1911, I told the Committee that this question of affiliation might come prominently forward; that there had been a great deal of criticism of the idea of denominational Universities, especially in so far as they cut across existing territorial jurisdictions; that the chief justification of the Aligarh University was that it would be a teaching as opposed to an examining university, that the young men who got their degrees and diplomas of the University would have imbibed the spirit of Aligarh which could not be acquired elsewhere. I again drew attention to the matter at a subsequent meeting held on the 27th of the same month. In an informal discussion with the promoters of the Hindu University, held at the Town Hall, Delhi, on the 4th December 1911, I clearly pointed out the difficulties which beset the proposal to grant affiliation. I mention this because there has been some misunderstanding on the point.

In order to meet the sentiment of the subscribers, it has been conceded that the University shall be called the Benares Hindu University. It will have no religious test and will be open to students of all denominations as well as to Hindus. Hindu theological teaching and observances will not be compulsory for any but Hindus. It will also be a teaching and residential University.

The terms mentioned above represent the conditions the acceptance of which is necessarily precedent to the elaboration of any detailed scheme. I hope that your Committee will realize that they are worked out in the best interests of the University and the Government, whose close association with it is essential. If they are not all that some of the subscribers may desire, they will enable you to realize an aspiration which a large body of opinion thought impracticable at the outset and which had been rejected by the Universities Commission of 1902. Should your Committee accept the conditions, details of the constitution can be settled. Sir James Meston will be at Allahabad on the 26th instant and will be ready to discuss the matter with us there.

I may add that His Majesty's Secretary of State reserves his final decision on the details of the constitution of the University until they are before him in the form of a draft bill and regulations.

In conclusion I have to state that when a satisfactory scheme has been evolved the Government of India will be glad to show their interest in the new University by making a liberal financial grant-in-aid. His Majesty's Secretary of State, the Government of India and the Local Government have only one object, viz., to assist your Committee to start this new and interesting experiment on lines best calculated to secure its success, and in so doing to cultivate and promote that enthusiasm for sound education which all who wish well to India whole-heartedly desire.

Yours sincerely,
Harcourt Butler

To

The Hon'ble Maharaja Bahadur Sir Rameshwar Singh, K.C.I.E., of Darbhanga"

Soon on 19 July, 1914, Sir Harcourt Butler sent a private and confidential letter to Darbhanga from Simla. A copy of this letter is given below[42]:

"My dear Maharaja Bahadur,

Herewith the letter in original with one hundred printed copies.

May I congratulate you on having carried the movement so far. I hope your people will be reasonable and that we shall soon work out a good scheme.

With all good wishes

Yours very sincerely,
S/d Harcourt Butler"

This letter indicates it clearly that higher officials of the Government at that time recognized only Darbhanga as the leader of the movement for the university.

Soon Darbhanga received a letter of J.H. Du Boulay, Private Secretary to Viceroy (dated the 22nd July, 1914) indicating the Viceroy's willingness to lay the Foundation of the University[43]. Subsequently, the Private Secretary of Jaipur wrote to Darbhanga on 26 July, 1914, congratulating him on the success of his efforts for the cause of the proposed University[44]. Then, in reply to Butler's letter of 18 July (mentioned before) Darbhanga wrote the following letter on 21 August, 1914[45]:

"Demi-official letter from the Hon'ble Maharaja Bahadur Sir Rameshwar Singh, K.C.I.E., of Darbhanga, to the Hon'ble Sir Harcourt Butler, K.C.I.E., C.I.E., I.C.S., dated the 21st August 1914.

As I informed you at Allahabad there is considerable apprehension regarding the terms and conditions laid down in your letter to me no. 22, dated the 18ᵗʰ July 1914. I think that if you would authorize me to place before the meeting of the 31ˢᵗ instant, informally, the substance of our conversation at Allahabad with Sir James Meston, Pandit Sundar Lal and Pandit Madan Mohan Malaviya, much of that apprehension would be removed, and the intentions of the Government of India would be more clearly appreciated. I refer particularly to paragraph 4 of your letter with special reference to the appointment of professors, the scope of inspection, the method of appointing examiners, the approval of the incorporation of local colleges in the University, the approval of the institution of new faculties and the reservation of power to lay down the limits of expansion at any particular time. I feel certain that the supporters of the movement would be genuinely grateful for a further pronouncement on these points before the meeting takes place.

Darbhanga referred to 'considerable apprehension regarding the terms and conditions" particularly in respect of the appointment of professors, scope of inspection, etc., among the supporters of the movement. However, Butler in his letter of 22 August, 1914, to Darbhanga, tried to explain and clarify the terms and conditions in detail. A copy of his letter is given below[46]:

"Demi-official letter from theHon'ble Sir Harcourt Butler, K.C.I.E., C.I.E., I.C.S., to the Hon'ble Maharaja Bahadur Sir Rameshwar Singh, K.C.I.E., of Darbhanga, no. 210, dated the 22ⁿᵈ August 1914.

I am obliged to you for your letter of yesterday's date. I have no objection to your placing informally before the meeting of your Committee of the 31ˢᵗ August, the substance of our conversation at Government House, Allahabad, under the Presidency of Sir James Meston. There has undoubtedly been misconception in certain quarters regarding paragraph 4 of my letter to you, which appears to be readily susceptible of removal.

2. In the first place I would point out that the words used in paragraph 4 of my letter were not intended to give more than the substance of the terms and conditions required. Verbal precision and definition must be left until the necessary enactment is drafted in the Legislative Department of the Government of India. I now deal with the terms of paragraph 4 of my letter seriatim.

3. The appointment of professors will be in the hands of the University. This was settled in the case of the proposed University at Aligarh and the Government of India have no intention of altering the procedure in the case of the Benaras Hindu University. The words "and such staff be appointed" referred merely to the power of the Chancellor to secure that the scale of staff was sufficiently strong for the objects of the University. I may point out that the necessity for such a provision is recognized in clause 9 (3) of the draft Hindu University Bill which was handed to me by the Honorary Secretary of your Committee on 23rd October 1912. I may add that the power of removal is explicitly given in the same clause.

4. The right of inspection or visitation is provided for in clause 9(1) and 12 of the draft Bill. The object of this condition is to secure that the standard of education is kept sufficiently high and that the University is run on lines generally approved.

5. Paragraph 4(c) of my letter contemplated leaving examinations in ordinary times entirely in the hands of the University authorities but reserved an emergency power to appoint examiners in the event of the standards of examination deteriorating. Clause 28 of the draft Bill provides as a regular procedure that at least one external and independent examiner shall be appointed for each subject or group of subjects. Should your Committee prefer such a rule with the condition that the appointment of the external and internal examines would be subject to the approval of the Chancellor, the Government of India, with the concurrence of

Sir James Meston, will recommend this modification of the terms to the Secretary of State.

6. The annual receipt of accounts – (d) of my letter; the approval of initial regulations, (f) of my letter; and the nomination of five members of the Senate – (h) of my letter; are directly or indirectly covered by the provisions of Clauses 16, 32 and 9(2) of the draft Bill.

7. Clause 10 of the draft Bill provided that the appointment of Vice-Chancellor should be subject to the approval of the Governor-General in Council.

8. The approval of the incorporation of local colleges in a teaching and residential University – (g) of my letter – is analogous to the affiliation of a college to an affiliating University. In the case of that latter the sanction of Government is required under section 21 of the Indian Universities Act, 1904.

Clause 19 of that draft Bill requires the sanction of the Governor-General in Council for the institution of new faculties. There is no intention to fetter the ordinary development of the University but new additions to the University would naturally require the approval of the Chancellor, who will necessarily be deeply interested in the growth and prosperity of the University.

I need scarcely add that in taking powers to intervene where necessary in the affairs of the University, the Government of India and the Local Government are animated by a desire to help a new experiment rather than to coerce it. It is far from their intention to crush initiative and enterprise on the part of the University authorities as some critics of the scheme appear to imagine."

On 9 September, 1914, Darbhanga wrote to Butler saying that he[47] was "still awaiting the draft of the formal reply of the University Committee." On 7 January, 1915, an official of the Department of Education wrote a letter to Butler that[48] *"Both Pandits Sundar Lal and Malaviya came to see me this morning. Both .... were most concerned that the final arrangement should be made in your time. I thought you might like to hear. Please don't reply to this."* It was probably clear by this time that Sir Harcourt Butler was being sent to Burma as Lt. Governor. This, perhaps, disheartened the members of the Society for Hindu University. On 11 January, 1915, Darbhanga wrote to Sir Butler that it[49]: *"will be impossible to come before February. My presence will scarcely be necessary during the drafting. I can come in February after the 7ʰ if you wish it. I am so sorry that you are going away early.*

I fancy that there will be very little opposition if any – but I am sure that a great deal of enthusiasm will evaporate by the news that its greatest supporter is going to leave the Education Portfolio. I had so hoped that you would go to the U.P instead."

On 11 January, 1915, <u>The Hindoo Patriot</u>, of Calcutta published the following report in the context of Hindu University movement[50]:

<u>The Hindoo Patriot</u>, **Vol. LXIII, No.2**
Calcutta, January 11, 1915, Page 2

"The Hindu University

The correspondence between Sir Harcourt Butler and the Maharaja Bahadur of Darbhanga, which has recently been published, has been read **with unmixed satisfaction by educated Hindus all over India**. It holds out a reasonably certain prospect of the Hindu University Scheme being materialized at no distant day. Verily, Sir Harcourt Butler could not have more appropriately signalized his relinquishment of the portfolio of education than by setting the seal of the approval of the Government upon a scheme the success of which has been the foremost in the thoughts of the Hindu community for the past few years. **In the Maharaja Bahadur of Darbhanga, the promoters have found a superb leader whose enthusiasm is equaled only by his influence and the future historian of the Hindu University will delight to dwell upon those highly successful tours of the Maharaja Bahadur from one end of the country to the other, which**

had brought such substantial accessions to its funds in all the successive stages of the movement. In his letter dated the 14th November last, the Maharaja Bahadur of Darbhanga wrote demi-officially to Sir Harcourt Butler expressing the gratitude of the Hindu University Society for a favourable decision as to the name and for the "very great interest" taken by the Government and for their liberal offer of grant-in-aid. The Society was however disappointed that its proposal that the Viceroy should be the Chancellor of the University should have been vetoed by the Secretary of State. Having regard however to the All India character of the proposed Hindu University, the Maharaja Bahadur went on to submit that it would not be quite in keeping with the dignity of the University to have the Lieutenant Governor as Chancellor, though the Society reposed the fullest confidence in Sir James Meston. Accordingly, the Maharaja Bahadur ventured to suggest, as an alternative proposal, that the Lieutenant Governor should be a Visitor, as in modern English Universities, that the University should be allowed to elect its own Chancelllor and that the powers proposed to be vested in the Viceroy should be exercised by the Government of India.

In his demi-official reply, dated the 23rd December last, Sir Harcourt Butler, speaking for the Government of India, wrote that he was very glad indeed to be able to assure the Maharja Bahadur that "there is now a bright prospect for a successful issue of our labours and discussion". He pointed out that nothing could be farther from the truth than to insinuate, as had been done in certain quarters, that the conditions imposed by the Government of India would "deprive the University of freedom and hamper its development". So far from this being the case, the Hindu University would in certain respects enjoy "more freedom than other Universities in India". For instance, to quote Sir Harcourt Butler's language, "it has been decided, to allow the University to elect its own Chancellor and the Vice-Chancellor, to appoint its own Professors, Lecturers and staff, to appoint its own examiners, and to conduct its own internal administration. Certain appointments will require approval and certain powers are reserved to the Government, but I anticipate that the normal work of the University will be conducted by the University itself exercising a large measure of independence. It is very far from the wish of Sir James Meston, the Government of India and his Majesty's Secretary of State to deprive the University of the privileges which are necessary for its dignity and usefulness". Under the arrangements proposed, Sir Harcourt Butler went on to point out, the Viceroy will be a Patron, while the Lieutenant Governor will be an *ex-officio* Visitor, vested with powers corresponding to those which the Government or Chancellor now ordinarily exercises in the existing Universities. The emergency power, which are of a purely precautionary character and sure to be most sparingly exercised, will rest with the Government of India.

We venture to think that this is an eminently satisfactory settlement and ought to be acceptable even to the most exacting. Governments and Governors have other things to occupy themselves with than to be perpetually finding fault with the working of a University of the *unique* character of the proposed Hindu University. The Government have indeed met the University Committee more than half way and after all ours is a world of comparisons and compromises. **We are indebted for these valuable concessions as much to the generosity of our enlightened Government as to the tact and sagacity of the Maharaja Bahadur of Darbhanga and the moderation and fairness of Pundit Madan Mohan, Dr. Sundar Lal and other prominent protagonists of the Hindu University movement.** The draft Bill submitted by the University Society will have to be redrafted, for, to again quote Sir Harcourt's language, "we should have to be guided eventually" so far as mere drafting goes, "by the expert advice of the Legislative Department of the Government of India". Then the amended Bill and initial regulations will have to be again submitted to the Secretary of State for his final sanction but Sir Harcourt does not anticipate any further difficulties and henceforth it will be all plain sailing.

In conclusion, we must congratulate Sir Harcourt Butler on the successful issue of this great scheme. His lengthy dissertations on different aspects of the educational problem, which he delighted in publishing from time to time in the guise of Departmental resolutions, laying down the programme for the next fifty years or so, may be forgotten. But his name will go down to posterity as that of the Education Minister during whose tenure of office the Hindu University scheme practically became all but an accomplished fact." (emphasis added)

This report gives a clear picture of the stages through which the movement of Hindu University had been steered so far. Butler's contribution has been precisely described. Besides, sufficient light has been thrown on the quality of leadership of Darbhanga and the extent of cooperation of Sundar Lal, Malaviya and other prominent supporters of the movement.

The Bill for Hindu University was introduced by Sir Harcourt Butler himself. Congratulating him for this Darbhanga wrote to him on 3 March, 1915[51]:

"your letter of the 25 instant. Just received. I am most grateful for your speech introducing the Hindu University Bill. I was not unprepared for Mr. Sitalwad's opposition.

In the Hindu Mahomedan conference we had at Allahabad some years ago with the Agha Khan in the chair Mr. Gokhle sat on the cross benches as he felt it his duty to be an Indian and not Hindu or Musalman. I presume Mr. Sitalwad wishes to follow in the same direction.... I had a letter from Mr. Lal.... Samaldas in which he says that although he was against the idea of a Sectarian University his doubts on the subject had been dispelled since."

Further, on 22 March, 1915, the Viceroy of India Lord Hardinge wrote to Sir Butler congratulating him[52] *"My very warm congratulations. Your speech was Excellent and its very conciliatory and friendly tone will I believe remove all ...... objections"*. The Statesman (Calcutta edition) published the full text of the speech of Sir Harcourt Butler Introducing the Bill For Hindu University. This is given below[53]:

The Statesman, March 24 1915

"Sir H. Butler's Speech"

Sir Harcourt Butler, in introducing the Hindu University Bill said:- My Lord, I move to introduce the Benaras Hindu University Bill. It is the earnest desire of the University Committee that this measure may be placed upon the Statute Book during the Viceroyalty of Your Excellency, with whose name University will be forever associated. It is but bare truth that without Your Excellency's constant interest, support and approval, this measure could not have been introduced today. By series of compromises the Government and the Society have arrived at conclusions which, I hope, may take the measure out of the domain of controversy. It is intended to publish the Bill now for general information to take the select community stage and pass the Bill into law during the September session. **Before I go further I must congratulate the Committee, and especially the Maharaja Bahadur of Darbhanga, Mrs. Besant, Dr. Sundarlal, Pt. Madan Mohan Malaviya, Rai Bahadur Ganga Prasad Verma, Sir Gooroo Dass Bannerji, Dr. Rash Behari Ghose, and outside the committee such active helpers as the Maharaja of Bikanir and the Maharaja of Benaras, on the success which has already crowned their efforts.** I need not review the history of the movement which resulted in proposals for the Hindu University at Benaras and the Moslem University at Aligarh, I will deal with the results that have emerged from long discussions. The facts are well known but I will confidently say this, that if anyone had predicted ten years ago, that the idea of University of this kind then in the air would take practical shape he simply would not have been believed. The University Commission, an influential body, had recently pronounced against such a University and there was a widespread opposition and hostility to any scheme which threatened to cut into the existing territorial and federal.... At the same time there is naturally a very little Knowledge in the country of what a teaching and a residential university is. To this want of knowledge I attribute much of the criticism which has been labeled against the constitution of the Benaras Hindu University.

The conditions which are appropriate and necessary in a teaching and residential university have been viewed awry through the glasses of mind habituated to existing universities. This is only natural in the circumstances of India. I wish it were possible to say in a few words what a teaching and residential university really means. Probably the best idea will be obtained from Cardinal Newman's idea of a University. May I quote a passage from the report of the Commission on University Education in London, the most authoritative statement of modern times of University Education? It runs as follows: In the first place it is essential that regular student of a University should be able to work in intimate and constant association with their fellow students, not only of the same but of different faculties, and also in close contact with their teachers. The University should be organized on this basis and should regard it as the ordinary and normal state of things. This is impossible, however, when any considerable proportion of students are not fitted by previous training to receive University education and therefore do not and can not take their place in the common life of the University as a community of Teachers and Students but as far as their intellectual education is concerned continue in the state (of) pupilage and receive instruction of mush the same kind as at school though under conditions of greater individual freedom. It is good that students should be brought together, if only in this way, and Cardinal Newman, writing in 1852 went so far as to say: "I protest to you gentleman, that if I had to choose between a so called university which dispensed with residence and tutorial superintendence, and gave its degrees to any person who passed an examination in a wide range of subject, and a university which had no professors or examinations at all but merely brought a number of young men together for three or four years and then sent them away, as the University of Oxford is said to have done some sixty years since, if we asked which of these two methods was better for the discipline of intellect which of the two courses were more successful in the training, moulding and enlarging of the mind, which sent out men more fitted for their secular duties, which produced better public men, men of the world, men whose names would descend to posterity, I have no hesitation in giving the preference to that university which did nothing over that which exacted of its members and acquaintance with every science under the sun."

Co-operation of Teachers and Students

Nevertheless this is only one side of the question and in any case Cardinal Newman does not refer to the kind of student life that can be reproduced in London. But, for this very reason, it is more essential that in such a university as London can have students and teachers should be brought together in living intercourse in the daily work of the university. From the time the undergraduate enters the University he should find himself a member of the community in which he has his part to play. Teaching and learning should be combined through the active and personal co-operation of teachers and students. The Association on more or less fraternal lines is the keynote of a teaching and a residential university and it does not aim at mere intellectual attainment overhung by examinations. It is the way of life and the way of corporate life. Those of us who have been at Oxford or Cambridge can appreciate the force and meaning of Cardinal Newman's vivid words. But Oxford and Cambridge are not the only models. There is much to be learned in India from other universities which are more definitely practical in aim. They are all, however, alike in this, that their outlook forms an atmosphere of concentrated thought and by friction of minds get truer perspectives, no matter whether the dominant note be philosophic or technic.

So much for the teaching and residential aspect of the university. There remains the question of religious instruction. Yet know the history of religious instruction in India, the fixed ………………….. account of the organization of the new university. You will see that it is a somewhat complicated organization and it has been necessary to define and adjust the functions with some care. The university is an All India university. It is incorporated for the teaching of all knowledge but will commence with five faculties – arts, science, law, oriental studies, and theology. I know that many of the promoters desire to add the faculty of technology. This desire has my full sympathy and I trust that adequate funds will soon be forthcoming. The university will be open to students from all parts of India on conditions which I shall specify hereafter. The Governor-General is Lord Rector and the Lieutenant Governor of the United Provinces of Agra and Oudh is the visitor of the University. Among those whom the university will delight to honour are patrons, vice-patrons and rectors. The governing body is numerous and very representative; the court with an executive body in council of not more than 30 members, of whom five will be members of the senate. The academic body is the senate, consisting of not less than 50 members, with an executive body in the syndicate. The senate will have entire charge of the organization of instruction in the university and its constituent colleges, the curriculum and examination, the discipline of students and the conferment of ordinary and honorary degrees. Except in matters reserved to it the senate is under the control of the court, working through the Council. The senate will be constituted as follows:- ex-officio (a) Chancellor, pro-Chancellor, vice-Chancellor and the pro-vice-Chancellor for the time being; (b) university professors; (c) principals or heads of constituent colleges of the university, 11 Elected (a) five members to be elected by the court; (b) five members to be elected by the registered graduates of the University from such date as the court may fix; (c) five representatives of the Hindu religion, and Sanskrit learning, to be elected by the Senate; (d) Should the vice-Chancellor declare that there is a deficiency in the number of members required in any faculty or faculties then five or less persons elected by the Senate, eminent in the subject or subjects of that faculty or those faculties; three nominated and five members to be nominated by the visitor. The syndicate will consist of a Vice-Chancellor Pro-vice-Chancellor and fifteen members of whom not less than fifteen members of whom not less than ten shall be University professors of constituent college. The object aimed at is to secure that purely academic matters should be decided by a body mainly experts, while the government (governance) and supervision of the university rests with the court and Council. It is necessary to represent the Senate on the latter in order that the academic view may always be before it. The Court will elect its own Chancellor and pro-Chancellor, vice-Chancellor and pro-vice-Chancellor. In the first instance these officers will be scheduled. The Vice-Chancellor will be ex-official chairman of the Council, Senate and Syndicate. He will be the chief executive officer of the university. The university will, through the council and board of appointments, appoint its own professors and staff and have entire control over them. Stability is given to its constitution by requiring the sanction of an external authority to changes in statutes and regulations. This is the outline of the constitution of the university.

Some Criticisms Met

The Government binds itself to accept degrees, etc., of this university as equivalent to degrees, etc., of existing universities. This in itself is no mean concession. My Lord, I have seen this constitution described as illiberal and I have rubbed my eyes in amazement. It is far more liberal than the constitution of the existing universities. No Government can allow universities to grow up without control. In most European countries universities, or at least the majority of them, are entirely State universities. In the course of these discussions two policies emerged. One was the policy of trust and the other a policy of distrust. The Government might well have said to society "You are starting a new kind of university without any experience in India. We must leaven it with officials who have the requisite experience. We must guide you from within, at any rate until you prove your worth and the value of your degree". That would not have been an unreasonable attitude. But we preferred to trust society, to leave them large autonomy, and to reserve to ....subject to the approval of the Chancellor. In the case of this University only 5 out of a minimum of 50 are nominated by the visitor who is ex-officio the Lieutenant Governor of the United Provinces, and this provision was suggested by yourselves in order to secure expert official help and co-operation. In Calcutta the appointment of professors requires the sanction of the Government of India. In this university no such sanction is required. There will be in this university under normal conditions no interference whatever from outside with the university staff. In Calcutta the vice-Chancellor is appointed by the Governor-General in Council. In this university the Court elects the vice-Chancellor, subject only to approval by the visitor. The Court has power to elect its Chancellor and pro-Chancellor. In the Court and Council the Government has no voice or representation whatever. Ordinary powers of intervention are vested in the visitor. The visitor will be close at hand. You will need his help at every turn in the acquisition of land and in many other ways. And you will not appeal to Sir James Meston in vain. Extraordinary powers are vested in the Governor-General in Council. You need not be alarmed lest they be exercised unduly. The tendency will be other way. It will not be in human nature that the visitor should seek lightly the intervention of the Governor-General in Council. I have not noticed such a tendency in local Governments. In the Government of India the tendency is all the other way, to avoid interference in details of administration. The terms are necessarily general but it is made quite clear that they are extraordinary and emergent powers, and, considering how much this movement already owes to the Government of India, I confidently ask you to believe in our *bona fides*.

We have trusted the promoters so much that I think we ourselves may claim some trust at your hands.

Admission to the University

So much for the constitution of the university. There remains the question of admission to the university and this raises the whole question of recognition of schools and matriculation. This will be dealt with in the regulations but I will tell you exactly what is our policy in this matter and what principles underlie it. Some of the promoters, I understand, desire to keep the recognition of schools in the hands of the University and to conduct their own Matriculation Examination. This wish is opposed to all the best modern view on the subject. The view strongly emphasized by the commission on University education in London that it is the central educational authority which is concerned to see that its grants are effectively used and that it is this authority also, which must provide for the co-operation of secondary schools and universities and must give necessary assurance to the latter that pupils seeking admission to their degree courses have reached the required standard of education. The Committee, I may mention, accept the recognition of schools by the local Governments and Durbars. As regards matriculation I must remind the Council that this is not a federal territorial university but a teaching and residential university. In the case of Dacca University the committee decided that it would not conduct its own matriculation examination. It was recognized that most of the high school students would be reading for admission to colleges of Calcutta University and that therefore the requirements of that university must regulate the course of studies. In those schools, in the case of the Benaras Hindu University, pupils of the high schools will similarly be reading for admission to the visiting universities and the new university could not with advantage set up a different standard or prescribe a new course. Again it was recognized that a separate entrance examination for Dacca, held at the headquarters of Dacca, would be cumbrous and difficult to carry out, and would be likely to cause confusion. These reasons are applicable with even greater force to Benaras Hindu University. Probably before many years have passed the external matriculation examination octopus, which digs its tentacles into all the limbs and parts of our secondary English schools, will be replaced by some system of school-leaving certificate. The most weighty authorities of times, the Consultative Committee on examinations in secondary schools, and Lord Haldane's commission on University Education in London, alike contemplate the abolition of purely external matriculation examination .... will come under reconsideration if at any time the school leaving certificate generally ousts the matriculation examination of other universities.

The Subscribers

I have now dealt fully and frankly with the two main points on which there have been differences of opinion. There remains yet another point on which there has been a misunderstanding that is easily removable. It is said that this University has ceased to be an All India University. This is not the case. It is open to students from every province and Native State in India. The school which is preparing for admission to it may be situated in any province or Native State in India. Its governing body is recruited from the length and breadth of India. It will send forth its *alumni* to every quarter of India. It will number among its patron Governors and heads of provinces, Ruling Chiefs and other eminent benefactors in all parts of India. I am informed that the following large subscriptions have already been paid: Maharaja of Udaipur 1.5 lakhs, Maharaja Holkar 5 lakhs, Maharaja of Jodhpur 2 lakhs, with a grant in perpetuity of Rs.2,000 a month, Maharaja of Bikanir one lakh with a grant in perpetuity of Rs.1,000 a month, Maharaja of Kashmir a grant in perpetuity of Rs.1000 a month, Maharao of Kota Rs. One lakh, Maharaja Bahadur of Darbhanga 3 out of 5 lakhs, Dr. Rash Behari Ghose 1 lakh, Dr. Sundarlal 1 lakh, Maharaja of Cossimbazar 1 lakh, Babu Brojendra Kishore Roy Chaudhuri of Gaureepur 1 lakh, and Babu Moti Chand 1 lakh. The Maharaja Scindia of Gwalior has promised five lakhs of rupees and others have promised liberal donations of which, in many cases, part payment has been made. If there ever was an All India University it is this. I think that on review of all the facts hon. Members will agree that the Government has dealt in a large and liberal spirit with the movement … conduct of negotiations has not been easy. It has been complicated by the fact that the movement started on line of its own without reference to Government and without knowledge of the conditions which Government considered essential to its success. It was further complicated by criticisms from opposing points of view. If to some it has seemed that Government was granting too little, to others it has seemed that Government was granting too much. I do not conceal from Hon. Members that in some quarters it has been considered that the Government was taking grave risks – risks graver than any Government ought to face. I can understand this view but I do not myself share it. We know that we are taking a certain amount of risk. We know that there is danger lest this University or similar universities elsewhere develop undesirable tendencies or lower standards of education. We deliberately face that risk, believing in the loyalty and good sense of India, and the growing desire to co-operate with Government on the part of the Hindu and other communities in India. For my part I am hopeful of success. I earnestly trust that the introduction of this Bill and removal of misunderstanding will lead to further enthusiasm and the provision of funds sufficient to build and equip the university on a worthy scale – a scale worthy of the great Hindu community. I confess that the other day, when I stood opposite Ramnagar, on the site where your university buildings will, I hope, soon be rising in stately array, and looked down the river Ganges to the ghats at Kashi, which swept before me in the distance, **I felt that if I was a Hindu I should be proud indeed of the achievement of my people, and at the same time I felt some little pride myself that I was a member of a Government which had joined in one more large endeavour to combine the ancient and honoured culture of India with the culture of the modern western world.**" (emphasis added)

Butler in his speech dealt with almost all the relevant issues, especially congratulated Darbhanga, Mrs. Besant, Sundar Lal, Malaviya, Ganga Prasad Verma, Gooroo Das Bannerji, Rash Behari Ghose and others in beginning and expressed his pleasure that "Government... had joined in one more large endeavour to combine the ancient and honoured culture of India with the culture of the modern western world" in the end. On 30 March, 1915, Gooroo Dass Banerjee sent a congratulatory message to Sir Butler in the following words[54]:

"I rejoice to find that the Hindu University Bill has been introduced into Council. Though we have not got all that we wanted, yet I hope what we shall get will afford safe and solid foundation for a true Hindu University which as it grows,

will dispel all apprehensions of the timid, and fulfil the best expectations of courageous statesmen like yourself.

We are deeply grateful to His Excellency Lord Hardinge, and to yourself, for your highly sympathetic and truly statesman like attitude towards the Hindu University Movement. And I may be permitted to add my feable voice to the chorus of approbation with which your speech when introducing the Bill has been received, a speech which for its noble thoughts and eloquent language will take rank as one of the most memorable speeches delivered in the Viceregal Council on the subject of Education."

On 16 June, 1915, C. Hill wrote to Darbhanga from Simla informing him that[55]

"His Excellency would prefer not to give any definite undertaking at present as regards the laying of the Foundation Stone in November, though, if circumstances permit, he will be very pleased to accede to your request. But the Bill has yet to be passed and various other preliminaries have to be gone through before the University can be regarded as <u>fait accompli</u> and the notification contemplated in section 1(2) of the Act can be published. It is necessary that the preliminary conditions specified in the first paragraph of Sir Harcourt Butler's demi-official letter No.202, dated the 13th July 1914, should be fulfilled, before I could take upon myself definitely to advise His Excellency to make a promise regarding the laying of the foundation stone; and, before I could give any indication as to the early opening of the University on a provisional footing which is indicated in your letter, I think that the Government of India ought to see the documents connected with the acquisition of the site and should have the assurance of the local Government that the arrangements for acquisition or purchase of the site are complete and satisfactory and that there will be no trouble in future in the matter of ownership. Secondly, as I verbally suggested to you, has not the time come when the accounts of your society ought to be properly audited and a report

made by a responsible authority to the Government of India? It is to be remembered that the five preliminary conditions were put before the Secretary of State as sine quo non preliminaries to the starting of the University at all.

The Government of India share your desire to secure the early opening of the University; but there is a point in this connection which I must bring to your notice. Notwithstanding the quotation you have given from Dr. Sundar Lal's letter you will have to consider very carefully whether the staff at the Central Hindu College, even when suitably strengthened, is at all sufficient for the purpose of a University. Here I dare say you will have some difficulty with some of the subscribers who may not realize the enormous difference which exists between the requirements of a college and those of a University. But the Government of India will of course do everything that can help you in the matter.

Mr. Sharp hopes to be able to get to Benaras during the rains. He tells me that at present he can make no definite arrangements by reason of the changes taking place in this Department but he will do his best and will gladly give you such advice as he can. I am doubtful however whether I could ask him to take upon himself to give full instructions as to what should be done before Lord Hardinge's arrival. As I have indicated above I think that His Excellency's visit to Benaras is bound to depend upon the progress made in the interim by the scheme; and although the Government of India would of course take into the most careful consideration any arrangements which might be drawn up by you and your committee in consultation with Mr. Sharp I doubt whether they could assume the responsibility for the initial organization. But this can be considered more easily when I have fuller information and when Mr. Sharp has looked thoroughly into the existing condition of things in Benaras."

Darbhanga, then, on 1 July, 1915, brought to the notice of Butler the letter he had received from C. Hill (given above) and informed him that he would again visit different places for collecting more fund for the University[56]. On 16 October, 1915, Darbhanga reported to Butler explaining the good response he had got in the second leg of his tour seeking financial help for the Hindu University. His letter is given below[57]:

> *"I came this afternoon after a most inconvenient journey. The Simla Mail was derailed; this caused some hours' delay and then my carriage was held off at Ambala for almost six hours and I had to be about thirty hours without food.*
>
> *The Meerut people had arranged a great reception and there is no doubt that that there is very strong feeling on the subject on behalf of both the Hindu and Mahemaden public. It was a very good thing that Government has taken the action that it has done – The problem before us now is to keep the movement well in hand so that Government and the ...... may continue to work in active cooperation. I know you will be able to solve it. I am to leave tomorrow after the meeting. I do not see whether the Aligarh meeting will come up. They have received very short notice and may not possibly be able to make the necessary arrangements. At Muzaffarnagar I am told Rs.30000/- were subscribed.*
>
> *I will write to you again after I have met Bikanir. I hope you have written to him."*

Subsequently, on 31 October, 1915, Darbhanga as the President of the Hindu University Committee, wrote to Butler inviting him to the Ceremony of Laying the Foundation of the University to be held on 4 December, 1915 in the following words[58]:

> *"May I as President of the Hindu University Committee be permitted to invite your Honour to the Foundation Stone ceremony of the 4 Dec. I am sure the Viceroy will give you leave and I need hardly assure you how welcome you will be to all members of the Hindu community. Sir Edward Gait will come and I believe from Simla's letter that Lord Carmichael will also come."*

Further, on 6 November, 1915, Darbhanga again reiterated his request to Butler in the following words[59]:

*"I shall feel obliged if your Honour will send me a wire accepting the invitation to the ceremony of laying the foundation stone of the Hindu University on Dec. 4th. Lord Carmichael, Sir Michael and Sir Edward Gait and Sir James Meston shall be there **but the ceremony will remain wholly incomplete without the presence of him who did so very much for us**. I am sure H.E. will give you permission. I will announce the acceptance in the papers as soon as I receive a telegram from you. Would you advise me to invite the Gov. of Bombay and Madras I may want as well take the chance. I am going to Bombay in Dec and will try to see the Governor personally. But your Honour <u>must come</u> you know how welcome you will be."*

But, it seems that the date of holding the Ceremony of laying the foundation stone of the University by the Viceroy was deferred. However, soon, by the end of January, 1916, it became clear that Banaras Hindu University would be established formally soon by the Viceroy. Butler, therefore, perhaps, sent the following telegramme on 2 February, 1916, only to Darbhanga congratulating him on the success achieved by him and others who had worked hard for it[60]:

Telegram
Rangoon to Benaras City

To
Hon'ble Maharaja of Darbhanga
Benaras.

I deeply regret that I cannot be present on the memorable occasion when His Excellency Lord Hardinge who has done so much for India and Indian education will lay the foundation stone of the Benaras Hindu University. I shall be with you in spirit. I congratulate you my dear old friend and all that great company of friends of yours and mine who worked so hard and so unitedly when things were not so easy as they are now to achieve what I think is perhaps the most interesting and significant movement of our time. I shall be thinking of you in the beautiful language of our 122nd. Psalm read in the spirit of sympathy and co-operation. Telegram

Lieutenant Governor. 2/2/16

Finally, the inauguration of Banaras Hindu University was held on 4 February, 1916. Lord Hardinge, who was Viceroy then came to formally inaugurate the University. Sundaram has given a detailed account of the ceremony in the following words[61]:

"On His Excellency's right hand were seated (1) Major-General His Highness Maharaja Sir Pratap Singhji Bahadur, G.C.S.I., G.C.I.E., Maharaja of Jammu & Kashmir, (2) His Highness Raj Rajeshwar Maharajadhiraja Sir Sumer Singhji Bahadur, Maharaja of Jodhpur, (3) Colonel His Highness Raj Rajeshwar Narendra Siromani Shri Maharajadhiraja Sir Ganga Singh Bahadur, G.C.S.I., G.C.I.E., LL.D., A.D.C., Maharaja of Bikaner, (4) Major His Highness Maharao Sir Umed Singh Bahadur, G.C.S.I., G.C.I.E., Maharaja of Kotah, (5) Major His Highness Maharajadhiraja Sir Madan Singhji Bahadur, K.C.S.I., K.C.I.E., Maharaja of Kishengarh, (6) His Highness Sawai Maharaja Sir Jai Singhji Bahadur, K.C.S.I., K.C.I.E., Maharaja of Alwar, (7) His Highness Maharawal Shri Sir Bijey Singhji Sahib Bahadur, K.C.I.E., Maharawal of Dungarpur, (8)His Highness Maharaja Lokendra Govind Singh Bahadur, Maharaja of Datia, (9) His Highness Maharaja Sir Prabhu Narain Singh Bahadur, G.C.I.E., Maharaja of Benaras, (10) His Highness Raj Rana Sir Bhawani Singh Bahadur, K.C.I.E., Raj Rana of Jhalawar, (11) His Highness Maharaja Ripudaman Singh Malwandar Bahadur, F.R.G.S., M.R.A.S., Maharaja of Nabha and (12) The Raja of Sohawal.

While on his left hand were:-

(1)His Excellency Lord Carmichael, Governor of Bengal, (2) His Honour Sir Jams Meston, Lieutenant-Governor of the United Province of Agra and Oudh, (3) His Honour Sir Michael O'Dwyer, Lieutenant Govenor of Punjab, (4) His Honour Sir Edward Gait, Lieutenant Governor of Bihar & Orissa, (5) Sir Shankaran Nair, Kt., (6) His Highness Maharaja Sir Rameshwara Singh

Bahadur, K.C.S.I., Maharaja of Darbhanga, (7) Sardar Daljit Singh, (8) The Hon'ble Dr. Sundar Lal Rai Bahadur, B.A., LL.D., C.I.E., (9) Dr. Deva Prasad Sarvadhikari, (10) Sir Gooroodas Banerji, Kt., (11) The Hon'ble Pandit Madan Mohan Malaviya, B.A., LL.B., (12) The Hon'ble Maharaja Sir Bhagwati Prasad Singh Bahadur, K.C.I.E., Maharaja of Balrampur, (13) Sir Prabha Shankar Dalpat Ram Pattani, and (14) Seth Narottam Morarji Gokul Dass.

In the blocks of seats beyond these on both sides were many other distinguished guests, Legislators, titular Rajas and Maharajas, Mahamahopadhyayas, Shams-ul-ulamas, Principals of colleges, a large gathering of the Trustees and Donors of the Benaras Hindu University, who had come together from all parts of the country, and all the most distinguished residents of Benaras.

As the notes of National Anthem died away, twelve little girls from the Central Hindu College Girls' School, who were under the guidance of the Principal, Miss L. Edgar, M.A., and were stationed on the steps leading down from the Viceregal chair into the amphitheatre chanted a short Sanskrit invocation, first to Ganapati, and then to the Goddess Sarasvati, a very fitting opening to the ceremony. The great Pandit, Mahamahopadhyaya Shiva Kumar Sastri, then came forward and uttered svastivachana shlokas, words of prayer for the blessing of God upon the work about to be performed, after which the **President of the Hindu University Society (Darbhanga), read the following address**:

"May it please Your Excellency,

It is my proud privilege today to respectfully offer to Your Excellency, on behalf of the Hindu University Society, a most cordial welcome to this ancient Seat of Learning, and to express our fervent gratitude for your gracious acceptance of our invitation to lay the Foundation-Stone of the Hindu University, which will ever remain associated, in the minds of the Indian People, with a Viceroy whose generous support and sympathetic encouragement have contributed so much to the realization of the earnest hopes and aspirations of Hindu India, which will now take concrete shape in this Institution.

The history of the movement for the establishment of the University, is briefly told. It carries us back to the year 1904, when, at a meeting held under the presidency of His Highness the Maharaja of Benaras, the proposal to found a Hindu University was first put forward. The idea took some years to mature, and led, in 1911, to the formation of the Hindu University Society, which was registered under that name. The Society was successful in obtaining the very next year, through the support of Your Excellency's Government, the approval of His Majesty's Secretary of State for India of the proposal to establish a teaching and residential University on the lines proposed. A short period of a little over two years, spent in the discussion of details, saw the Benaras Hindu University Bill passed into law and placed on the Statute Book of the Land on the first of October, 1915.

It is a source of deep gratification that the idea has effectively touched the hearts of the people of the land. The great and noble Princes, the landed gentry and the general public, have all come forward as one body to generously support the movement. Their contributions to the University Funds now amount to close upon one crore of rupees, including the capitalised value of the annual grants, sanctioned by Ruling Princes, to which Your Excellency's Government has been pleased to add an annual grant of a lakh of rupees. The selection of a suitable site, affording full facilities for the ever-progressive development of a great University, growing and expanding with the growth of ideas and ideals, as well as of the multifarious demands and needs of modern life and its many sided activities, was the first measure which engaged the attention of the Society, and the site on which we are assembled today, extending over more than 1200 acres, was selected after much consideration.

The incorporation of the Central Hindu College in the new University had been contemplated from the beginning, and, **thanks to the ready co-operation of Mrs. Annie Besant and the other Trustees of the College, whose labour of love and devotion had built up that institution, the College has been transferred to the Society to serve as the nucleus of the University.** The movement reaches its culminating point today, when we are met to witness the Foundation of the University being laid by Your Excellency.

The reasons which demanded the establishment of such a University may also be briefly stated. It is impossible to recall the state of education which existed in India at the beginning of the British rule and compare it with the stage it has now reached, without a sense of deep gratitude to the Government which has brought about this momentous change. Great also is our indebtedness to our existing Universities which have contributed in so large a measure to the diffusion of higher education among our people. But these Universities are, at present, mainly examining bodies, and there is an ever growing consensus of opinion that those Universities also can best discharge their high functions and fulfil their mission which teach as well as examine, which impart not only literary but also scientific and technical education combined with research, and which mould the character of their alumni by helping them to live their academic life in healthy environments, under the personal influence and loving care of good and capable teachers.

There was another equally powerful reason for inaugurating this movement. While we highly appreciate the value and need of education in European Arts and Sciences, we cannot divest ourselves of the consciousness that we have inherited a culture and civilization of our own, which reaches further back in time than that of any other people, and which possesses, as we believe, in a special degree the elements of social stability as well as the fundamental principles of physical, intellectual and spiritual progress and welfare. Amidst all the vicissitudes through which Hindu society has passed, it has, in all essentials, clung to that civilization and has ever been governed by it. There was naturally a widespread desire in our community that we should have a central educational institution of our own, to preserve and promote our distinctive civilization and culture, and to instruct our youth in the sacred precepts of our religion. The promoters of the University believe that if our students are brought up in our traditions and culture and instructed in the precepts of our religion, they will grow up into men of vigorous intellects and high character, who love their Motherland, are loyal to the King, and are in every way fit to be useful members of the community and worthy citizens of a great Empire.

Deep, therefore, is our gratitude and great our joy that, under the dispensation of a benign Providence, with the generous support of the Suzerain Power of the Rulers of Indian States, and of the public, we witness here today the foundation of a great Institution, which seeks to combine the usefulness and efficiency of the modern system of education, with the high spiritual ideals of ancient India.

This auspicious day will ever remain memorable in the history of our country. Never before perhaps in that history did the highest representative of the Sovereign and the Rulers of so many States and Provinces meet to co-operate with the people to bring into existence an educational institution like the proposed University. The gratitude that we feel towards Your Excellency is too deep for words, for our success is in the largest measure due to the generous sympathy and support which the movement has received at Your Excellency's hands. Nor should we omit to express our obligations to the Hon'ble Sir Harcourt Butler for his valued advice and friendly help at every important step in our progress. We are also deeply thankful to the Rulers of Provinces and Indian States, who have honoured and encouraged us by their presence. Equally grateful are we to the distinguished scholars and educationists, who have, by so kindly responding to our invitation, given us an assurance of their guidance and co-operation in the great task that lies before us of building up an Ideal University and making it in every way worthy of the continued patronage and support of all well-wishers of this land.

We take this opportunity of expressing our gratitude to all subscribers to the funds of the University, particularly to Ruling Princes and other principal donors, who have helped us with liberal contributions.

Time will not permit of our mentioning the names even of all donors of large sums, but we may be allowed especially to express our obligations to His Highness the Maharana of Udaipur, His Highness the Maharaja Gaekwad of Baroda, His Highness the Maharaja of Mysore, His Highness the Maharaja of Jammu & Kashmir, His Highness the Maharaja of Jodhpur, His Highness the Maharaja of Jaipur, His Highness the Maharaja Scindia of Gwalior, His Highness the Maharaja Holkar of Indore, His Highness the Maharao of Kotah, His Highness the Maharaja of Bikaner, His Highness the Maharaja of Kishengarh, His Highness the Maharaja of Alwar, His Highness the Maharaja of Nabha, His Highness the Maharaja of Benaras, His Highness the Maharaja of Kapurthala, His Highness the Raj Rana of Jhalawar, His Higness the

Maharaja of Datia among the Ruling Princes, and to the Hon'ble Maharaja of Darbhanga, the Hon'ble Maharaja of Cossimbazar, Sir Rash Behari Ghose, Thakur Suraj Buksh Singh of Sitapur, Babu Brajendra Kishore Roy Choudhury, the Hon'ble Babu Moti Chand and Dr. Sundar Lal, who have each contributed one lakh or more to the funds of the University.

We also desire to thank the Government of India for the handsome grant of one lakh a year. We fully realize that we require a much larger sum than we have yet been able to secure. But we have every hope that the generous public will help us with all the funds we need to build up this new and great Temple of Learning.

Your Excellency's administration, which we are grieved to think is drawing to a close, will ever be memorable for the spirit of true and active sympathy with our national sentiments and aspirations and for an earnest endeavour to appreciate and satisfy popular needs. Many are the wise and beneficent measures which have distinguished Your Excellency's Viceroyalty.

Among these, the support you have given to the cause of education, in general, and of higher education, in particular, the inauguration of residential and teaching Universities and the liberalization of educational policy by sanctioning the establishment of a private University, will stand out conspicuous and be gratefully cherished in the memory of the people. These measures have won for Your Excellency the deep admiration and grateful affection of all classes and sections of the community, and have secured for you a highly honoured place in the history of our land. As a memento of the deep and kindly interest which Your Excellency has taken in the Hindu University, the Jodhpur Darbar have endowed a Chair of Technology, with an endowment of Rs. 24,000 a year, which they and we desire to associate with your honoured name, and we crave Your Excellency's permission to our doing so. That endowment will, we hope, serve as a nucleus for the development of the Faculty of Technology of the University in the near future.

We are also deeply indebted to His Honour Sir James Meston for the keen personal interest he has taken in our work; and we take this opportunity of expressing our gratitude both to him and to the officers of the Government for the invaluable assistance and co-operation we have received from them in making the requisite arrangements for this function.

We cannot conclude without giving special expression of our gratitude to H.H. the Maharaja Sir Prabhu Narain Singh of Benaras for the paternal interest he has taken in and the fostering support he has always extended, from the very beginning of its life, to the Central Hindu College and to the scheme of the University itself, and last but not least for the liberality of his co-operation in arranging for the reception of our distinguished and honoured guest on this occasion.

I now humbly request Your Excellency to be pleased to perform the great ceremony which has brought us here today, and we fervently pray to the God of all nations that He may bless the great work Your Excellency is about to inaugurate, so that it may fulfil, in ever greater and greater measure, its pure and noble purpose of welding together the noblest culture of the East and of the West, and that He may vouchsafe health and happiness to Your Excellency, peace and prosperity to this ancient land and to the great Empire of which it forms a part, and long life, glory, and power to the noble and gracious King-Emperor who rules over this Empire."

The address was placed in a beautifully engraved silver casket, fashioned to represent a temple of Shiva, and was presented to His Excellency by Sir Gooroodas Banerji. The Viceroy then made the following reply:

H.E. the Viceroy's Reply

"It has seldom fallen to my lot to address a more distinguished gathering than that which I see before me today, including, as it does, the Governor of Bengal, a constellation of Lieutenant Governors, a veritable galaxy of Ruling Princes, and so much of the flower of India's intellect. What is it that has brought together this brilliant assemblage from so many distinct parts of Hindustan? What is the lodestone that is exerting so powerful an influence? It is there in front of us, a fine block of marble, but little different in outward appearance from many others that I have helped to set in their places during the past five years. But, in spite of its apparent simplicity, it possesses a deep

88

significance, for it betokens a new departure in the history of education in India, and one that has attracted the most intense interest on the part of all good and thoughtful Hindus. This Foundation-stone will mark a definite step in the advance towards an ideal that has stirred to its very depths the imagination of India. The demand for enlightenment and educational progress grows ever stronger, and the ceremony we are gathered here to perform offers some small response to that demand and may perhaps pave the way for its more rapid fulfillment. To such an audience as I have before me here, it is unnecessary to enlarge upon the need for providing greater facilities for University education of this country. We all know or have heard of the pressure that exists in our existing University centres; of the enlargement of classes to unwieldy dimensions to admit of the inclusion of the ever-increasing number of students; of the melancholy wanderings of applicants for entrance from college to college when all colleges were already full to over-flowing. There is a great division of opinion between the advocates of quality, and there is much to be said for both. The charge is frequently brought against Government that they are too eager for quality and too ready to ignore the demand for quantity, and comparisons are made, that do not lack force, between the number of Universities in England, America, and other countries, and the number available to the 300 millions of India. Nevertheless, it is the declared policy of the Government of India to do all within their power and within their means to multiply the number of Universities throughout India, realizing, as we do, that the greatest boon Government can give to India is the diffusion of higher education through the creation of new Universities. Many, many more are needed, but the new Universities to be established at Dacca, Benaras and Bankipore, soon to be followed, I hope, by Universities in Burma and the Central Provinces, may be regarded as steps taken in the right direction. Here, at any rate, in this city, is a case where we can all stand together upon a common platform, for no one can dispute that the Benaras Hindu University will add to the facilities for higher education and relieve to some extent the pressure of existing institutions, while it is proud boast of at least one of those who have so successfully engineered this movement, that the degrees of the Benaras Hindu University shall be not only not lower but higher in standard than those of existing Universities. It has even been claimed that this University will only justify its existence when the education given within its precincts shall make it unnecessary for Indian students to go to foreign countries for their studies, and when such expeditions will be limited to advanced scholars and professors, who will travel abroad to exchange ideas with the doctors and learned men of other Continents, in order to make the latest researches, and all branches of knowledge available to their own alumni at Benaras.

That is a great and noble aim; and if it is fulfilled, as I hope, it may be, this University will satisfy the claims alike of quantity and quality; and I think all will admit that Government have not been backward to give their co-operation and assistance to a scheme so full of promise. But this University is going to do something more than merely increase the existing facilities for higher education. Its constitution embodies principles that are new to India, in that this is to be a teaching and residential, as contrasted with an affiliating and examining, University. I am not ignorant that these principles have already secured general acceptance from most thoughtful men, but they were not fully recognized when our older Universities were established, and they can only be partially applied to their constitutions. Perhaps I was wrong to say that these principles are new to India, for though in ancient times there was nothing quite like a modern University, its prototype may be dimly discerned in the far distant past, and the tradition that comes down to us is one of thousands of students gathered round such great teachers as Vashishtha and Gautama; and, indeed, the whole Indian idea of education is wrapped up in the conception of a group of pupils surrounding their "guru" in loving reverence, and not only imbibing the words of wisdom that fall from his lips, but also looking up to him for guidance in religion and morality and moulding their characters in accordance with his precept and example. To this and similar schemes my Government have consistently given their support, and I and my advisers came to the conclusion at an early stage in the history of the movement that it would be wrong and impolitic on the part of Government to resist the desire shown by the Hindu and Muhammadan communities of India to inaugurate special Universities of this new type. But, whether the idea of a residential teaching University be new or old, there is no doubt that it is a departure from the existing model, nor is this the only departure that characterizes this enterprise. Indeed, I do not myself think that, important as the distinction may be, it is going to have so great an influence upon generations yet unborn as that other departure that the constitution of this institution embodies, and that is indeed of the very essence of its creation. I mean its denominational character.

There are some who shudder at the very word 'denominational', and some who dislike new departure of any kind. Controversy has raged round such points in England, and educational problems have a way of stirring up more feeling than almost any other social question. I do not think this is unnatural; for their importance cannot be exaggerated. If you realize that the object of an educational system must be to draw out from every man and woman the very best that is in them, so that their talents may be developed to their fullest capacity, not only for their individual fulfilment of themselves, but also for the benefit of the society of which they find themselves members – if you realize this, is it not well that men should strive with might ... to obtain and be content with only the very best, and is it not natural that the strife should produce a mighty clash of opinion and conviction?

But, the questions at issue cannot be settled by theory and discussion. Education is not an exact science, and never will be. We must also have experiment; and I for one consider that Lord Ripon was a sagacious man when he deprecated that the educational system of this country should be cast in one common mould, and advocated, as he was never tired of doing, that variety which alone, he urged, can secure the free development of every side and every aspect of national character. I should like to remind you, too, that this new departure of a denominational University is not quite such a novel idea as some of you may think, for the Education Commission appointed by Lord Ripon, while recognizing that the declared neutrality of the State forbids its connecting the institutions directly maintained by it with any one form of faith, suggested the establishment of institutions of widely different types, in which might be inculcated such forms of faith as the various sections of the community may accept as desirable for the formation of character and the awakening of thought. They recognized the danger that a denominational college runs some risk of confining its benefits to a particular section of the community. And thus of deepening the lines of difference already existing. But I am not terrified by the bogey of religious intolerance; rather do I think that a deep belief in and reverence for one's own religion ought to foster a spirit of respect for the religious convictions of others; and signs are not wanting that the day is drawing, when tolerance and mutual goodwill shall take the place of fanaticism and hatred. That Commission touched with unerring finger the weakest spot in our existing system; for, though something may be done by mental and moral discipline and something by the precept and example of professors, these are but shifting sands upon which to build character, without the foundation of religious teaching and the steadying influence of a religious atmosphere. My own personal conviction, strengthened by what I have seen in other lands, is that education without religion is of but little worth. That, then, is the great idea that has brought you all together to witness the ceremonial inception of this experiment. Here, you hope, in the not far distant future, to ee preserved and fostered all that is best in Hindu ideals of life and thought: all that is noblest of Hindu religion and tradition, culture and civilization, and grafted upon that tree, healthy and strong in its own natural soil, you hope to see growing in it and of it, all that is good and great of Western science, industry, and art, so that your young men may go forth, not only inspired with pure and noble ideals, but also equipped for the development of their mother country along the more material lines of progress and prosperity.

As regards the actual constitution, this has been a matter of prolonged negotiation with the promoters of the University movement and with the Secretary of State. Into the history of the negotiations it is not necessary for me to enter. I need merely observe that my Government have throughout been animated by one main purpose, to leave the greatest possible freedom to the University, consistent with its development on such safe and sound lines as would be approved generally by the Hindu community. I feel confident that the promoters of this scheme will zealously see to the right conduct of this institution. I am glad to think that I shall leave the University in the capable and sympathetic hands of Sir James Meston, who is your first Visitor. The position of Visitor is one of dignity and influence, and I know that you will always be able to rely on Sir James Meston for wise help and sound advice. We have not arrived at the present stage without a considerable amount of effort and hard work, and **I should like to take this opportunity of expressing my high appreciation of the zealous, but reasonable, spirit in which the Maharaja of Darbhanga, Pandit Madan Mohan Malaviya, Dr. Sundar Lal, and others,** on behalf of the promoters of the University, conducted negotiations with Sir Harcourt Butler as representing the Government of India, to whose great tact and conciliatory attitude I believe the promoters of the scheme would pay as high an eulogy as I wish to pay myself, and thus enabled the measure which gives birth to this institution to be passed through my Council in time of war as a non-controversial measure. **I also tender my most hearty congratulations to the**

Maharaja of Darbhanga, Pandit Madan Mohan Malaviya, and other members of the deputation that spent so much time and labour in enlisting the sympathy and generosity of their countrymen for this scheme. I watched with greatest interest their wanderings from city to city, and noted the welcome they everywhere received and the enthusiasm of their audiences. "Heaven helps those that help themselves"; and the result is that they have succeeded in collecting a sum that guarantees a commencement upon a sound financial footing, and justifies us in taking today this first step towards putting the scheme into material shape. We have heard the names of many of those who have contributed with princely liberality to make this possible, and the Benaras Hindu University should never forget how much she owes to the Ruling Chiefs of India. But much more will be required in the future to secure the early completion of all the requisite buildings, and I trust that the generosity of the great Hindu community may be like an ever-flowing stream to feed this Fount of Learning. What will be wanted even more than money, is really competent professors and teachers; so let me make this appeal to the whole of Hindu India to send her best men from every quarter here, so that they may help to create a true University atmosphere, and thus make this great experiment a great success. The Act which we passed last October has still to be put into force, and I am glad to announce that the necessary steps are being taken to do so at an early date. I trust that when the University has been thus brought into legal existence, every care will be taken to proceed with due deliberation and circumspection, so as to ensure that the quality of the instruction given and the surroundings in which it is imparted, may be worthy of the great position which this University aspires to attain.

To my friend, His Highness the Maharaja of Benaras, special gratitude is due, for not only does the Central Hindu College, which is to form part of the nucleus of the new University, owe much of its life and inception to him, but he is also making concessions in connection with the acquisition of the land for this great new experiment; and where could a Hindu University be more happily placed than here in Benaras, the ancient Seat of Learning, clustered about with a thousand sacred associations? Here, if anywhere, should be found that religious atmosphere which seems to me so essential to the formation of character, and here, if anywhere, the genius of modern progress will be purified by the spirit of ancient culture. But it is my earnest hope that those who have done so much to bring this scheme to fruition, will not now rest upon their oars. For the moment, provision will be made by the transfer of the existing Arts, Science and Oriental Departments of the Central Hindu College to the University, so that facilities for teaching these subjects may be supplied. I understand also that His Highness the Maharaja of Jodhpur, in addition to a lump sum grant, has promised an annual grant of Rs.24,000, which may render possible the inauguration of the study of some special technical subject. And I accede with pleasure and pride to the request that has just been made that my name should be associated with the Chair of Technology, which it is proposed to found with that endowment. But, I trust, you will not let your ambitions be satisfied with this, but will steadily keep before you the aim of creating Colleges or Departments of Science, of Agriculture, and Commerce, and Medicine, so that the Benaras Hindu University may be a place of many-sided activities prepared to equip young men for all the various walks of life that go to the constitution of modern society; able to lead their countrymen in the path of progress; skilled to achieve new conquests in the realms of science, art, industry, and social well-being, and armed with the knowledge as well as the character so essential, for the development of the abundant natural resources of India. Let it be our prayer that this stone may contain within it the germs of all that is good and beautiful and wise for the enrichment of the educational system of India, the enlightenment and happiness of her people, and the glory of God." (emphasis added)

"After this, His Excellency went to the central dias, amidst a shower of flowers from the little girls, and performed the ceremony of laying the foundation-stone, which had the following inscriptions on it:

BANARAS HINDU UNIVERSITY
THIS FOUNDATION-STONE WAS LAID
BY H.E. THE RIGHT HONOURABLE
CHARLES BARON HARDINGE OF
PENSHURST,
P.C., G.C.B., G.M.S.I., G.C.M.G., G.M.I.E.,
G.C.V.O., I.S.O.,
VICEROY & GOVERNOR-GENERAL OF INDIA
FEBRUARY 4, 1916

It is obvious from the above mentioned account of the inauguration ceremony that speeches were delivered by only two persons, namely, Darbhanga and the Viceroy. The latter in his inaugural address mentioned first the name of Darbhanga and then the names of Madan Mohan Malaviya and Sundar Lal appreciating their efforts and congratulating them on their success. Darbhanga was thus recognized by the Viceroy too as a central figure along with Malaviya, Sundar Lal and others in the movement for the University. It may be pointed out that Butler had also sent his congratulatory message (by telegramme of 2 February, 1916) only to Darbhanga. He replied to Butler on 7 February, 1916, (soon after the inauguration) in the following words[62]:

*"*Telegram

Benaras City to Rangoon
7/2/16

To Lt. Governor, Rangoon.

On behalf of the Hindu University and my own I send our most grateful thanks for your extremely kind message and the invaluable support and sympathy from you which has resulted in the creation of the University.

Maharaja Darbhanga"

Notes:

1. Sundaram, V.A. op.cit p.93
2. Ibid, p.93
3. Ibid, p.94
4. See File No. MSS EUR F116/70, British Libraries, London
5. This document is preserved in the Kalyani Foundation Archives. A scanned copy of it is given on Appendix-6
6. See File No. MSS EUR F116/70, British Libraries, London
7. Ibid,
8. This letter is preserved in the Kalyani Foundation Archives. A scanned copy of it is given on Appendix-7
9. See File No. MSS EUR F116/70, British Libraries, London
10. This letter is preserved in the Kalyani Foundation Archives.

11. A copy of the letter of Rameshwara Singh and a copy of the circular of the General Manager are preserved in the Archive of Kalyani Foundation

12. "ismaili.net/sultan/smspg2.html"

13. See His Highness the Maharaja of Darbhanga – An Appreciation, 1916, Ganesh & Co., Madras, p.16, included in Jha, Hetukar ed. 2010, op.cit, p.304; See the letter of Saiyid Zahiruddin, Member, Bengal Legislative Council, to The Hon'ble Mr. H. Le Mesurier, Chief Secretary to the Government of Eastern Bengal and Assam, dated the 18th January, 1912, included in Jha, Hetukar ed. 2010 op. cit, p.187

14. See File No. MSS EUR F116/70, British Libraries, London

15. Ibid

16. Ibid

17. Ibid

18. This letter is available in the Archives of Kalyani Foundation. A scanned copy of it is given on Appendix-8

19. This report is available in the Archives of Kalyani Foundation. A scanned copy of it is given on Appendix-9

20. The document in this context is preserved in the Archives of Kalyani Foundation. A scanned copy of it is given on Appendix-10

21. See File No. MSS EUR F116/70, British Libraries, London

22. See File No. MSS EUR F116/70, British Libraries, London

23. The letters of Jodhpur (25 December, 1912), Bhabnagar (3 February, 1913), and Kapurthala (19 March, 1913) are preserved in the Archives of Kalyani Foundation. A scanned copy of it is given on Appendix-11

24. Sundaram, V.A., op.cit, pp 110-114

25. A copy of this report and that of the letter of Darbhanga are preserved in the Archives of Kalyani Foundation. A scanned copy of it is given on Appendix-12

26. Sundaram, V.A., op.cit, pp 119-128

27. This letter is available in the Archives of Kalyani Foundation. A scanned copy of it is given on Appendix-13

28. In this context see Darbhanga's letter to Butler of 17 June, 1913; 22 June, 1913 and Butler's reply of 24 June, 1913. All these three letters

are preserved in the File No. MSS EUR F116/70, British Libraries, London

29. This report is published in Jha, Hetukar ed. 2010 <u>A Liberal Hindu Aristocrat, Maharajadhiraja Rameshwara Singh of Darbhanga</u> (1860-1929), <u>op.cit</u>, p.17

30. This letter and the accompanying report are preserved in the Archives of MKSK Foundation. A scanned copy of each is given on Appendix-14

31. This letter is available in the Archives of Kalyani Foundation. A scanned copy of it is given on Appendix-15

32. See File No. MSS EUR F116/70, British Libraries, London

33. See File No. MSS EUR F116/70, British Libraries, London

34. A copy of the report of this meeting is preserved in the Archives of Kalyani Foundation. A scanned copy of it is given on Appendix-16

35. This letter is preserved in the Archives of Kalyani Foundation. A scanned copy of it is given on Appendix-17

36. This letter is available in the Archives of Kalyani Foundation. A scanned copy of it is given on Appendix-18

37. See File No. MSS EUR F116/70, British Libraries, London

38. See File No. MSS EUR F116/70, British Libraries, London

39. See Ghosh, Suresh Chandra, "Introduction", p.5 in Suresh Chandra Ghosh ed. 1977, <u>op.cit</u>

40. See File No. MSS EUR F116/70, British Libraries, London

41. This letter is preserved in the Archives of Kalyani Foundation. A scanned copy of it is given on Appendix-19. Further, scanned copy of Pioneer's report of 24 July, 1914, is given on Appendix 19A.

42. This document is preserved in the Archives of Kalyani Foundation. A scanned copy of it is given on Appendix-20

43. This document is preserved in the Archives of Kalyani Foundation. A scanned copy of it is given on Appendix-21

44. This document is preserved in the Archives of Kalyani Foundation. A scanned copy of it is given on Appendix-22

45. This document is preserved in the Archives of Kalyani Foundation. A scanned copy of it is given on Appendix-23

46. This document is preserved in the Archives of Kalyani Foundation. A scanned copy of it is given on Appendix-24

47. See File No. MSS EUR F116/70, British Libraries, London

48. See File No. MSS EUR F116/70, British Libraries, London
49. See File No. MSS EUR F116/70, British Libraries, London
50. A scanned copy of this Report is given on Appendix-25
51. See File No. MSS EUR F116/70, British Libraries, London
52. See File No. MSS EUR F116/70, British Libraries, London
53. A scanned copy is given on Appendix-26
54. See File No. MSS EUR F116/70, British Libraries, London
55. See File No. MSS EUR F116/70, British Libraries, London
56. See File No. MSS EUR F116/70, British Libraries, London
57. See File No. MSS EUR F116/70, British Libraries, London
58. See File No. MSS EUR F116/70, British Libraries, London
59. See File No. MSS EUR F116/70, British Libraries, London
60. See File No. MSS EUR F116/70, British Libraries, London
61. Sundaram, V.A., op cit, pp 252-277
62. This report is available in the Archives of Kalyani Foundation. A scanned copy of it is given on Appendix-25

Chapter 3

Epilogue

The historic mission of establishing Hindu University in Benares, thus, came to be fulfilled. The letters and speeches of the top authorities of Government (mentioned before), Darbhanga's efforts for collecting fund (for the University) from different corners of the country (narrated before) and the confidence of the members of the Society for the Hindu University reposed in him by unanimously reelecting him as the President of the Society (described before), suggest, rather explicitly, that Darbhanga remained in the forefront as the central figure leading the movement from 1904-05 to 1916. Besides, the records and proceedings of the meetings held from time-to-time (cited before) reveal in no uncertain terms what Mrs. Besant, Malaviya, Sundar Lal and others also did for the success of the project of the University. One may, under the circumstances, consider at least three persons (namely, Darbhanga, Mrs. Besant and Malaviya) to be sharing the credit of being the Founders of the Banaras Hindu University in 1916 with the help and support of Sundar Lal and others. In any case, Darbhanga's role in this context can hardly be supposed to be second to that of anyone else.

Sundaram, however, describes that a copper plate having inscriptions in Sanskrit and English declaring Malaviya as the only "prime instrument" (that is, the only leader) of the movement was placed in a cavity under the "marble-stone"[1]. It is not clear whether the said cavity was (is) under the Foundation-Stone (laid on 4 February, 1916), or, some other "marble stone". Further, another question that arises here is regarding the time when the said cavity was made and how and by whom the copper plate was placed in it. Since this event has not been even slightly mentioned in the proceedings of the inaugural ceremony (of 4 February, 1916), nor in the reports of Sundar Lal, it may be presumed that the said cavity was possibly made sometime later for containing a copper plate having an inscription highlighting simply the role of Malaviya. The relevant passages (of the English version) of the inscription are given below[2]:

"...**The prime instrument of the Divine Will in this work was the Malaviya Brahmana, Madan Mohan, lover of his motherland. Unto him the Lord gave the gift of Speech, and awakened India with his voice, and induced the leaders and the rulers of the people unto this end.**

And other instruments also the Supreme fashioned for His purpose – the high-minded and valiant Ganga Sinha, Ruler of Bikaner; the noble Rameshwara Sinha, lord of the lands of Darbhanga, the President of the Assembly of workers and bringer to it of honour; the wise counsellor, Sundar Lal, learned in the law, the storer of the treasures and the keeper of the secrets; and sages like Guru Dasa and Rasa Vihari and Aditya Rama, and also the lady Vasanti of the silver tongue, Elders of the land, full of tenderness for the younger generation. And other Servants of the Lord served in many ways..."

Thus, the inscription on the copper plate celebrates Malaviya's name as "the prime instrument" and sizes up Darbhanga, Mrs. Besant, Sundar Lal as mere "Other instruments". It seems to have projected Malaviya's name alone as The Founder of the Banaras Hindu University. The history of the movement from 1904-05 to 1916 was thus superseded by the said inscription. Chattopadhyaya (Mukherjee), however, it seems, justifies this supersession and has tried to explain it in terms of conflict/competition between aristocracy (represented by Darbhanga) and middle class (represented by Malaviya) in which the latter gained upper hand as Malaviya[3] "was recognized by the nation as the chief architect and father of the Banaras Hindu University". This appears to be somewhat a rash assumption. One fails to discern how the entire "nation" came forward to recognize Malaviya as the Founder of the University in her account. Besides, if Malaviya is supposed to be the leader of middle class of all those who were not rajas/zamindars, what can be said about Sundar Lal, Gooroo Dass Bannerji, Professor Radha Kumud Mukherji, Professor Benoy Kumar Sarkar, Ras Behari Ghose and other members of the Management Committee of the Society for Banaras Hindu University who unanimously reelected Darbhanga as the President of the Committee? Following Chattopadhyaya (Mukherjee)'s understanding of 'class', the said persons may also be supposed to be of the same (middle) class, who, however, remained behind Darbhanga. It seems that mere dependence on 'class' consideration in this context can hardly be appropriate for understanding or analyzing the totality of interrelationships of social, political and religious/cultural forces which dominated the social reality of India in the beginning decades of the last century. One may contend here that post-establishment events relating to Banaras Hindu University deserve to be the subject of a separate research.

Regarding Darbhanga, it may also be noted here that he was keen to protect and promote the interests of Hindus in general without losing sight of those of his Muslim brethren. According to a report published in <u>Indian Review</u>[4] in 1912 "He was the President of Bihar Hindu Association, the Punjab Hindu Sabha was also established under his guidance and inspiration. He collaborated with Babu Sarada Charan Mitra to bring into existence the All India Hindu Association. It was at his suggestion that His Highness Agha Khan consented to hold Hindu-Mohammadan Conference at Allahabad in 1910… In fact, he is the leader of Hindus throughout India…" It has been mentioned before that he contributed a handsome amount to the fund of Aligarh Muslim University. In the Conventions of Religions held in Kolkata in 1909 and in Allahabad in 1911, he eloquently spoke for promoting tolerance, Hindu-Muslim unity and for getting rid of the practice of untouchability (described before). The Government at that time had no project of establishing any denominational university. Rameshwara Singh, however, came forward for tactfully persuading the top authorities (such as Butler) to consider the project of Hindu University.

Without the approval of Government, how could it be possible for one (person or class) to establish a Hindu or Muslim university? It was in the interest of Hindus in general regarding their cultural and educational traditions, and not in his own material interest, that Darbhanga devoted all his energy to the Hindu University movement. Even in the inaugural speech of Viceroy (4 February, 1916, given before), one finds that his name was first among the few who were congratulated by him (Viceroy) on their success. It seems that his entire contribution (of money, time and energy) was ignored after the establishment of Banaras Hindu University. The verdict of later years, thus, appears to be virtually in defiance of history.

Notes:
1. Sundaram, V.A., op cit, pp.277-283
2. Ibid, p.281
3. Chattopadhyaya (Mukherjee), op cit, p.334
4. Ibid, p.301, fn.18

Appendix

श्रीविश्वनाथा जयति ।

Sri Sarada Viswavidyalaya.

(WITH CIR. Nᵒ 44)

A PLEA FOR THE ESTABLISHMENT OF
THE NUCLEUS OF A HINDU
UNIVERSITY TO BE KNOWN AS SRI
SARADA VISWAVIDYALAYA.

For private opinion.

The Hindus in former days were well-known for their high morals and other virtues such as devotion, obedience and loyalty etc. They were contented yet energetic and plodding, peaceful yet brave, dignified without conceit, happy without luxury, and devoted, obedient and loyal without show and display. They were kind parents, dutiful children, sympathising neighbours, charitable hosts and loyal subjects. They had always lived and acted on the maxim "simple living and high thinking."

But we do not find now the same virtues, the same spirit of self-sacrifice, the same devotional and moral nature amongst their descendants.

Why it is so ?

The simple answer "change of time" is not sufficient. Time no doubt has very powerful influence over everything, but time alone is not responsible. It is our own actions—that make us fit to the time—that are also answerable for this change. If we look calmly into the thing, we will find that it was proper education and training that made the Hindus what they were and it is the want of those, that has made them what they are now. So long as *Varnasrama Dharma* of the Hindus played a prominent part in their domestic, social, religious and high educations in life, so long the Hindu character, the Hindu thought and the Hindu nature were moulded into a type that had produced the most remarkable peace-loving, contented, religious, brave yet saint-like specimens of the past. The more the education had changed its course and the more it became distant from the higher ideals of *Varnásrama Dharma*, the greater we have fallen off from our goal. It would not be too much to say that, it is the *Varná-srama Dharma* only that has yet kept up the Hindu name, the Hindu Society and the Hindu nation. Many a powerful nation has passed away unnoticed from the face of the earth after playing their splendid parts in the arena of this great stage, but yet the survivors of the great Hindu nation, however degenerated they may have become, have kept up the light and have prevented the falling of the drop scene.

There is not the least doubt that Western education and the Western knowledge and learning have their incalculable benefit in the life pilgrimage of the man, but the question is,—Does the adoption or the adaptation suit us better. The present tendency is, the adoption of everything Western; but this tendency, so far as it has been successful, has diverted the Hindus very far from their own ideals and what the result is, it is needless to mention. If we substitute want for plenty, anxiety for peace, indifference for action, perfidy for devotion, misery for happiness, luxury for simplicity, disobedience for dutifulness, impertinence for liberty, conceit for modesty insubordination for loyalty,—then we can realise the consequence of adopting the Western everything at the sacrifice of the Eastern.

Those, who yet desire to pull down mercilessly the great tower of the *Varná-srama Dharma* built up after millions of years of experience by the giant Hindu hands of yore, ought to bear in mind that their tiny little strength is entirely incapable of substituting any thing permanent in the place of the old. At the present moment, Hindu progenies, full with the Western cults and thoughts, with spades and other instruments of destruction at their hands, are energetically engaged with all the fervour and strength of their mind to pull down piece by piece the adamantine structure of the *Sanatan Varndsrama Dharma*. They sincerely believe in their mind that this *Varnasrama Dharma* stands as a great obstacle on their way to make speedy progress in the march of national and racial evolution; but our honest belief is that those who entertain such ideas cannot commit a greater mistake, a more serious blunder than this. Greatness of a nation lies in its own inherent qualities, even as the greatness of a person rests upon his own qualifications. No one has ever become great by giving up his own and adopting that of others; if such were not the case, then why we, inspite of our so much adoption of Western, are not called great, and why the world both old and new, even the best and most learned of them, cherish the memory of our ancestors the simple and the contented Hindus, with all reverence and admiration—nay even bow down before their scriptures and like worthy pupils devote themselves to their study and consider it worth their while to meet the expenses of sending out agents for unearthing and collecting ancient but neglected manuscripts of the old Hindus This proves unquestionably that the path we have decided to follow in adopting Western line in education and other matters, is not the line of safety and prosperity for us. Our decision ought to have been to keep everything of our own holding on tenaciously to our old ideas and old methods of simple life so far the present times allow us to do, while like devoted students, we try to acquire all that is good great and beneficial in the Western education. If we pursue this, our course is safe, our path steady and future glorious; but if we fail in this, howsoever we may try to imitate the West by putting on their borrowed plumes, we will never be able to rise in the scale of humanity as a true, real and great Hindu nation.

The revival of education on *Varnasrama Dharma* and the scriptures and philosophy from Vedas, *Upanisadas*, down to *Puranas* tory from the time of the advent of the British rule in India they have got this most auspicious occasion of Imperial visit to their mother-land. Therefore where could a better opportunity be offered for the establishment of the nucleus of their University than to do it now in commemoration of His Imperial Majesty's Coronation visit to this our sacred land.

THE KIND OF VISWAVIDYALAYA WE PROPOSE TO ESTABLISH.

India is a vast continent and therefore any idea of centralised education would not suit people living in different distant provinces. The people are generally poor and would not be able to bear all the costs of a centralised university education. The proposed University of the Hindus therefore will have very little of Western method of centralisation. We do not require to found any costly colleges after the Western fashion in any particular Province of India. But we wish to utilise the *Pathsalas* and *Vidyalayas* existing in and within the jurisdiction of the great centres of ancient learning. In olden times India had several seats of learning (Vidyapithas) such as Kashi (Benares,) Kashmir, Navadwip, Ujjain, Nasik, Mithila, Kanchi, Ishtava, Punyapattan, Muttra and other places. They are all now more or less discouraged and neglected,—the result being that the high-class teachings from those centres of learning are fast disappearing. If we can revive those Institutions, help them in their tuition and point out a method of teaching that would be free from the defects of old Eastern and new Western systems, we believe we have done something towards the proper education of the Hindu mind.

Another feature of this University will be the elimination of the system of competition. In old days they never knew anything like competition : it is the idea of competition that produces jealousy in the mind, that afterward results with the maxim " survival of the fittest," a most inhuman, a most unnatural idea that

2

could have ever generated in the human mind. Is God Almighty only for the fittest ? Is human being—the intelligent man—still in the brute creation where only the animal nature prevails to fulfil the maxim—"survival of the fittest"? Any sedate observation would show that though the great nature allows this in her grossest form she is all just and merciful in her nobler aspect. It is we, who try to degenerate and demoralise her by importing lower order into higher sphere. India was *all* prosperous because there was no idea of the survival of the fittest. Every one found his own place according to his own capacity. If there was that glorious system of joint family, it was because there was no poisonous seed of competition instilled into the ears of the young. If there was that life-imparting system of *Varna* and *Asrama* that have still kept up the spark of life in Hindu body, it was because there was no idea of "Survival of the fittest" known amongst the Hindus. If Hindus never knew selfishness and luxury it was because they were taught to supply the want of others before they fulfilled their own. Thus, we find that the cancer of selfishness generated by the poison of competition is actually eating up the Hindu hearts and making the Hindus a shadow of the real man. We cannot, therefore, foster the idea of competition in the minds of the young students, when we see its painful effect in their juvenile hearts. We can see it clearly in its most unhealthy expressions and horrible aspects in the different countries of the West where the actions of the votaries of this goddess—the victims to the monster of competition and its natural corollary—the survival of the fittest—might someday bring havoc in the administration of the Western Empires.

Another speciality of the method of imparting knowledge in this University would be "want of compulsion." After a very preliminary general education every subject will be made optional with the student who will be quite at liberty to

select one or more according to his taste,
capacity and inclination of mind. When
all subjects are compulsory in a system of
education up to a very high degree, no
solid knowledge of every subject can be
expected from each and every student.
The great learned scholars of the olden
days could not have become authorities in
the subjects they have treated if they had
to spend half of their lives in acquiring
knowledge of compulsory subjects against
their inclinations. Thus we find that some
best intellects do not find scope to display
their knowledge, being saddled with this
compulsory system. It is not only a loss
to the individual but also a very great loss
to the society and to the cause of learning.
A flint, that strikes sparks without multifarious admixtures, is many times more
solid and durable than a match that composed of various ingredients ignites but
once only on the box.

Another speciality will be that there
shall be no defined text books for students of
higher standard, they shall increase their
knowledge with the help of libraries, laboratories and professors. Test of their
competency for receiving degrees, titles and
diplomas &c., will be the recommendation
of their respective professors.

Another speciality of this Viswavidyalaya would be to impart technical education.
This should be given in a grand scale and
in all its departments after the Western
system with all its latest improvements.
First it would be given to those who by
their long line of heredity are most fitting
receptacles to receive it. If past India has
had unparalleled success in all kinds of
technical education it was because it was
imparted to fit subjects according to the
rules of the Varnasrama Dharma. There
cannot be a greater mistake—a more serious
blunder than to impart such education indiscriminately. A son of a carpenter, a
goldsmith, a silversmith, a shoemaker etc.
can learn the professions of their respective
ancestors much sooner than others. It is a
mistake to make a *Brahmin* a *Vaisya* by

profession unless he has a natural inclination for it. It is the seed, the blood that coming down from a long line of ancestors play a most important part in building up the taste, the tendency and the inclinations of a man, and we ought to welcome such things when they exist ready-made in a country like India. Other countries have no such heredity-producing system amongst their inhabitants, consequently an anomaly of selecting professions exists among them. A shoemaker's son becomes a missionary and the descendant of a missionary takes to the profession of a cobbler. But those who have their lines of heredity systematised from time immemorial, it would be a rank mistake for them not to take advantage of it. Indeed it would be greatly beneficial to impart technical education keeping in view the order of Varnasrama Dharma so far as it may be possible. Let not people think that any particular class or *Varna* be depressed or that any order should be bound down hard and fast by any narrowness of mind. A full and a fair play to be given to those in all matters of technical education, so that all classes may work hand in hand and side by side as parts of a harmonious whole like what they did in golden days of India.

Another feature of this University would be that tuition so far as it is possible will be imparted in the different vernaculars of the people while Hindi and elementary English should be kept as a compulsory subjects. It is believed that there would be no difficulty in carrying out this plan because each centre of learning will have the facility of the local dilect while recourse will be taken to English when it will be found absolutely necessary to do so.

Another speciality of this University would be the comparative study of the knowledge of East and West such as that of Astronomy, Astrology, Medicine, Botany and similar subjects.

Another speciality of this University would be the compulsory teaching of Hindu scriptures. Each sect should be primarily taught his own scriptures in their own schools without fanning the sectarian hatred and bigotry. This can only be done by adopting a particular line of tuition in which the fundamental unity in the doctrines of all the sects will be properly explained, till the students have reached the higher standard of philosophy of the ancient Rishis.

Another feature would be that so far as it may be possible, after the old system of *Brahmachari Asrama* and *Gurukul Nivas* in each centre of learning, there will be provided places for the living and boarding of students according to *Varnasrama Dharma*.

Each centre of learning will, as far as funds permit, be equipped with an observatory and scientific laboratories etc., to carry on teaching as well as research work in various branches of science.

The female education will also be given as far as possible according to the *Varna-srama Dharma* keeping in view the technical education of various kinds that are fitted for the Hindu girls.

SUBJECTS TO BE TAUGHT.

Higher studies in Sanskrit on different subjects that are to be pursued in each centre will vary in accordance with the local needs and traditions of each centre of learning and therefore a curriculum of studies should be hereafter drawn up after consultation with the scholars of each centre of learning so as to meet the proper requirements of each place.

But the course of studies will embrace the teaching of the Vedas, of the philosophies and of the sacred books of the Hindus besides literature, science and arts which include all sorts of technical education to the different Varnas, so as to make them superior craftsmen in their line. This will be fixed after due consideration keeping in view the various requirements with the consultation of the experts concerned.

3

TEXT-BOOKS

The text-books for the general use of students of the primary schools and second class colleges will be prepared by the Central University Council. But special text books to suit provincial needs will be chosen and prepared as will be found necessary by the authorities of each centre of learning with the help of other scholars, experts and educationists subject to the approval of the Central University Council.

It will be one of the chief objects of the University to enrich the Hindi language by increasing its stock with the translation of various subjects from English and other languages and also by comparative research in both science and literature and other subjects.

ORGANISATION.

There should be two different sections in the organisation. Sri Sarada Mandala is the Central Council of this Viswavidyalaya. The number of members in it for the present shall be limited to fifty, with power to add, and they are to be elected by the different centres of learning, by the Dharmacharyas (Religious Heads) of different Sampradayas, by the patrons, by the representative body of the Sri Bharat Dharma Mahamandal and by the fellows and supporters of the University. The Council will have a President, two Vice-Presidents and as many Secretaries as may be found necessary. The Sarada Mandal being the Vidya Bibhaga of Sri Bharat Dharma Mahamandal, the General President of the latter body will have chief voice in controlling the financial matters of the University.

The Council will have power to make rules for its own guidance to hold executive meetings &c., and do all that is necessary to manage, control and conduct each and every of its departments as well as the different centres affiliated to it

Similarly there will be local councils of education in each centre of learning with their Presidents. Vice-Presidents and Secretaries. These councils will have full power to make rules for their respective guidance in all local matters connected with the subjects under their control. But such rules shall not be in any way repugnant, contradictory and inconsistent to the rules made by Central Council.

The University will commence its work at Benares which will be the Headquarters of the Central Council of the University and the Benares centre of learning will be first revived.

AFFILIATION.

Each centre of learning will have power to affiliate Pathsalas (Tols), Vidyalayas (second class colleges), Mahavidyalayas (first class colleges) and other educational institutions under its jurisdiction.

EXAMINATION.

There will be examinations for all technical subjects and also for primary and second class education. Such examinations will be held at each centre annually, and rules for the guidance &c. of such examinations will be framed by the centre of each learning with the approval of the Central Council of the University.

TITLES, &c.

Titles, Diplomas &c. will be conferred and given by this University to the worthy, deserving and successful scholars by the Central Council of the University at a convocation. The Diplomas &c. for the primary schools and second class colleges will be granted to the successful students who will pass the examination from their local centres.

FUNDS NECESSARY.

If the work of this University is carried on the lines as contemplated it is deemed that a very large amount of fund will not be, necessary at least to begin work with. Centralisation perhaps requires crores but this simple method of utilising the existing institutions and commandeering the reputed

traditional Seats of Learning Vidyapithas undoubtedly will not require even
one-tenth of that amount.

The most novel and inviting feature
of this idea is that the centres of learning
being local institutions in various parts of
the country, the people residing within
the sphere of influence of each centre will
not only like to take special interest in the
matter but it will be comparatively more
gratifying to them and consequently easier
to raise funds for its support. In a vast
continent like India the people of Tuticorin
would scarcely care to take interest for a
college that may be established according
to the method of centralisation in such a
distant place as Kashmir ; but if they have
their own centre in their own part, they
will assuredly take more interest in the
matter. To every body his own dialect is
naturally dear ; so it also gives him greater
facility to acquire knowledge than through
a foreign language to him. Consequently
he would like to support an institution
that would impart knowledge to his children through his own dialect.

So far the scheme has been thought of
at present. The support and maintenance
of each Vidyapitha (Centre of Learning)
will rest on the help of the people interested in that particular centre. But now the
question is when each centre will be thus
supported by its own supporters, how the
central organisation of Sri Sarada Mandal
(Benares) will be maintained. To this the
reply is, by the contributions from different
Vidyapithas and by its own income to be
derived.

It will be comparatively easy to collect
funds for the other Vidyapithas when once
the central organisation of the University
and Kashi Vidyapitha are properly established, and there is also a very great hope
that some Vidyapithas may be maintained
by the local chiefs and particular Sampradayas (Religious sects).

The funds necessary for establishing a
Central Council at Benares and to com-

mence work at the local (Benares) Vidya.
pitha may be estimated at Rs. 25,00,000
twenty-five lakhs of rupees—the details of
this expenditure may be given hereafter.
If we can raise this amount and begin work
at Benares we can fairly hope to commence
successfully work in other Vidyapithas
almost immediately. It is not the work of
the day in which success can be achieved.
We believe in the gradual development
and therefore we work on the line of
evolution and not revolution.

Why we have estimated the commencement of work at such a small amount is
because we will be able to utilise many
other resources which lie at our command
by the virtue of its being the *Varnasrama
Dharma* University.

APPEAL.

If the exemplary Hindu life and higher
ideals to be preserved for the future generations, if the ancient philosophy of the
Rishis—unparalleled in the annals of the
world's history be revived in their supreme
grandeur and glory, if the solemn debt
which the Hindus owe to their ancient sages
(Rishi-rin) for knowledge attained be dis-
charged with the feelings of gratitude in-
born in Hindu minds, if the all-embracing
Hindu religion that takes in its vast catholic
bosom all the grades and shades of Hindu
order and imparts four-fold blessings to
them be saved from the hands of destruction, if the spiritual giant, the prodigy of
valour and strength, the symbol of prosperity and wealth and the specimen of service and work be again produced by the ancient machine of Varnasrama, if Hindu home
should again ring with the joyous sound of
the Vedas and Hindu hearth enjoys plenty
and peace, then no more time should be
wasted and opportunity neglected, yet the
Hindus have not lost the breed of their
noble blood, the greatness of their heart
and energy of their action. Yet the Hindu
charity and benevolence stand like living
monuments in all parts of India and pro-
claim with iron tongue the noble deeds
of the worthy ancestors of our present

4

chiefs, noblemen and gentries ; and will
not the scions and descendants of those
glorious forefathers, the sons of traditional
houses, the gentries of good reputation and
fame, the representatives of religious
orders, the founders, the preceptors of
different Sampradayas and Panths and the
great Hindu public that form the bulwark
of Hindu faith, the life of Hindu religion
and strength of Hindu society, now come
forward with munificent hands to serve the
noble cause of their own religion, philosophy and material improvement ? Will
not they like to see their ancient glories
revived and their nation march on the
healthy line of peace, prosperity and spiri-
tuality, and will not the paternal Government come forward to help such a noble
movement ?

We sincerely hope—they will.

Thri
Gurhwal

16/9/11.

My Dear Maharaja Sahib,

I have the pleasure to inform you that Swami Gyananand ji, while on his way to Badrinath, stayed here for about a week, and during this time I have had a long discussion with him re the proposed Hindu University. I also read in the papers the condition which you consider sine qua non and I am glad to say that I fully concur with you. Time has arrived when the Western Education must not be given indiscriminately but must be tempered with religious instructions. There has been enough of impiety in the past and the consequences have been simply horrible and unless something is done to check the trend further, serious mischief will be inevitable.

As you are the head of the Bharat Dharma Mahamandal and consequently of all the Hindus, I hope you will be able to do something in the matter and earn the gratitude of all true Hindus.

With best regards,

Yours Sincerely

H.H. Maharaja Rameshwar Singh Bahadur, K.C.I.E.,
President of the Bharat Dharma Mahamandal,

118

At a public meeting in connection with the Hindu University held at Meerut on 17th October 1911 H. H· the Maharaja Bahadur of Darbhanga who occupied the chair said :—

Gentlemen I heartily thank you for the cordial reception you have accorded to me and the members of the Hindu University deputation and for the honour you have done me in asking to preside at this gathering. The question of a Hindu University has long been in the air. Many years ago the idea presented itself to the Bharata Dharma Mahamandala. My friend, the Hon'ble Panit Madanmohan Malviya, has been long working at it with his usual energy and unrivalled power of organisation. You are aware, gentlemen, that several projects, more or less crude, have been put forward for the favourable consideration of the public. I was convinced, however that before Hindus could draw up any complete scheme which would be generally acceptable, it was absolutely necessary to get some indication of the wishes of Government on the Subject.

2. In a conversation I had at Allahabad in Jully with Pandit Madanmohan Malviya on the subject, I told him that I would attend public meetings in support of the cause after I had been assured that the scheme would receive the support of the Government of India and that ample facilities would be afforded for the study of the religion of our forefathers under the auspices of the leader of the Sanatana Dharma. It was there decided that I should approach the Government and ascertain its views. I came to Simla in August with this object but was informed that the question was under the consideration of Government and that it would take some weeks to get a reply. I returned to Simla last week, and have had an opportunity of discussing the matter with my friend, the Member for education. I am now in a position to tell you, gentlemen, that the response has been most favourable. Our lasting gratitude is due to His Excellency the Viceroy and to the Hon'ble Member for education for the very kindly personal interest which they have taken in the matter. I shall have the pleasure of laying before you the correspondence that has passed between me and the Hon'ble Mr. Butler and I am convinced that you will consider it eminently satisfactory. He has most kindly agreed to receive a deputation at Delhi after his return from Bombay when we are to discuss informally the details of the scheme with him. I understand that the Hindu University will not identify itself with any sect or creed but will impart religious teaching to boys in accordance with the religious forms professed by their fathers or their guardians. I do not believe that Hinduism is

hopelessly divided into different irreconcilable creeds and sects. On the contrary I take it that on essential points we are agreed. Our sacred religion lays down rules of proper conduct. We call it Dharma common to all, although different ways and methods have been prescribed by our Rishis to suit people of different temperaments and environments, but all eventually lead to the Almighty. The idea is extremely well expressed in that very well-known Stotra of Pushpdanta.

त्रयी सांख्यं योगः पशुपतिमतं वैष्णव मिति
प्रभिन्न प्रस्थाने पर मिद मदः पथ्य मिति च ।
रुचीनाम्वेचिभ्या ट्टकुटिल नाना पथ जुषां
नृणामेको गम्य स्त्वमसि पयसा मर्णव इव ॥

Vidya, as understood by our ancestors represented much more than mere secular learning. It meant knowledge and right action based on such knowledge. True education, then, should not stop with physical and intellectual training but should extend to the spiritual. It should prepare boys for the work and for the careers that they have to follow as well as enable them to gain mastery over their lower natures and to fit them for the higher life. Anarchy and sedition can find no place in a society where education is regulated on such principles. Our Rishis foreseeing the danger of one-sided development provided for the cultivation of the intellect as well as that of the soul. Rules of conduct were held to be as useful and obligatory as knowledge of books. The one was considered to be a necessary complemet of the other. It has been truly said by a European savant that Hindus eat religiously and sleep religiously. I hold that an education which does not provide for instruction in the religion of one's forefathers can never be complete and am convinced that a Hindu will be a better Hindu, a Christian a better Christian, and a Mohammadan a better Mohammadan, if he has implicit faith in his God and in the religion of his forefathers. I have never believed in a godless education and have invariably advocated the necessity of combining secular education with religious training. I join in the movement for the University in the earnest hope that it will produce this happy combination and that the boys whom it shall turn out will be God-loving, truthful, loyal to their Sovereign, devoted to their country, and fit in every way to take their place in the great future that lies before them.

I have now much pleasure in reading to you, gentlemen, the correspondence that has passed between the Hon'ble Mr. Butler and myself.

My dear Mr Butler,

You are aware that there is a wide-spread feeling amongst the Hindu public to establish a Hindu University on such lines as may be approved and sanctioned by the Government of India. More than one project has been put forward in this connection, but I think it very necessary, before any further action is taken in the direction of producing a complete scheme which will be generally acceptable to the Hindu public, that we should first try to obtain from you a clear indication of the lines on which Government will be prepared to support the idea of a Hindu university. I am quite convinced that Hindus will be only too happy to loyally carry out any directions that Government may be pleased to give them and will thankfully accept any suggestions that you may be pleased to make.

I hope that you will very kindly place this letter for the favourable consideration of his Excellency, the Viceroy.

Your very Sincerely,

(Sd) Rameshwara Singh.

My dear Maharaja Bahadur,

I have received your letter of the 10th instant in which you refer to the wide-spread movement amongst the Hindu public to establish a Hindu University on such lines as may be approved and sanctioned by the Government of India, to the different schemes put forward, and to the desirability of my making a pronouncement as to the lines on which Government will be prepared to support the idea of a Hindu University. You add that you are quite convinced that Hindus will be only too happy to carry out layally any directions that Government may be pleased to give them and will thankfully accept any suggestion that I may be pleased to make.

You will understand that in the absence of definite and detailed schemes it is not possible for me at present to do more than indicate certain conditions, on which the Government of India must insist as antecedent to the recognition by Government of a movement for the establishment of a Hindu University. These are—

(1) The Hindus should approach Government in a body as the Mohammadans did ;

(2) A strong efficient and financially sound college with an adequate European staff should be the basis of the scheme;

(3) The University should be a modern University, mainly in being a teaching and residential University and offering religious instruction;

(4) The movement should be entirely educational;

(5) There should be the same measure of Government supervision and opportunity to give advice as in the case of the proposed University at Aligarh.

I need scarcely add that it would be necessary hereafter to satisfy the Government of India and the Secretary of State as to the adequacy of the funds collected and the suitability in all particulars of the constitution of the University. The Government of India must of course reserve to itself full power in regard to all details of any scheme which they may hereafter place before the Secretary of state whose discretion in regard to the movement and proposals that may arise from it they cannot in any way prejudice

I may add that the Government of India appreciate the spirit of the concluding passage of your letter, and that you can count on the ungrudging co-operation of myself and the department in furthering any scheme that may commend itself to the Government of India and the Secretary of State.

Yours Sincerly,
(Sd) Harcourt. Butler.

Printed by Matroo Lal at Arya Bhushan Machine Press Meerut

Private   Dehradun

                                    31 October 19..

My dear Mr Butler,

            Many thanks for your letter of the 24th
which I received on my return to Dehradun.

            Mrs. Besant grasped the situation
at once.

            I saw Pandit Madan Lal at
Benares but could get no opportunity to
have a private talk with him. I am

124

afraid however that you will have some difficulty
in getting him to fall in with your views.
Sir John Hewett was not very sure about
his willingness. However there is plenty of
time to think about this question and I have
no doubt that matters will be all right
in the end.
            Malaviya writes to me to accompany
a deputation to Bikanir & Gwalior. I
am writing to him that it will be best to

want on after the Delhi Darbar. I have
also written to His Highness of Dikanis to the
same effect. I think that it will be just as
being his Chiefs were to to join after you
have an opportunity of talking to them.

I have received several suggestions to the
effect that it will be an excellent thing if His
Majesty were to say a few words expressing his
pleasure at the invitation of the two Universities.
Personally I am sure that Hindus & Mahomedans
will be delighted at such an expression of

His Majesty's permission & May I suggest that you would mention this subject to His Excellency if you agree with me —

I leave Darrough on the 13th. and shall be in Calcutta — & shall then meet — until the 27th. November. Will you kindly send me your own programme.

I was told in Benares that the 2nd & 3rd Dec would suit them better than the 30th November. Will you kindly let me have a word. Would you like to me to send you a list of the members that they propose to form the Deputation.

Please send to me any suggestions or restrictions that you may consider necessary and I will do my best to carry them out.

Yo gratefully,
Rameshwara ——

Confidential

Druvaaya

8 November 1911

My dear Mr Darke,

Many thanks for your letter... I thought it would be rather a difficult matter but was sure that you would be able to do it and was not surprised when I received Malaviya's telegram, at the same time that I received your letter, to the effect that Sunder Lal has accepted the Principalship. We have nothing now but to proceed forward. I see from that you have agree to the 3rd December, being the date of the deputation. I have told Macaulay that Chiefs are to come into the scheme after the Deputation was over. He wished me to go to Bikaner & Gwalior in deputation but both the Maharaja & myself have advised him to postpone it till after the majority leaves India.

I hope to be in Calcutta next Monday.

Yours very sincerely

Rameshwara Singh

129

HINDU UNIVERSITY MEETING.

At a meeting held on Wednesday, 17th current, in the Calcutta Town Hall to promote the Hindu University Scheme, H. H. the Maharaja of Darbhanga, President of the Hindu University Committee, in proposing that H. H. the Maharaja of Bikanir do take the Chair, said :—

I have much pleasure in proposing that H. H. the Maharaja of Bikanir do take the Chair. Such an act on his part may be taken as an indication of his warm interest in the scheme we have in view and is also, I take it, a clear indication of the feelings of all the other Ruling Chiefs throughout India towards the establishment of a well-equipped Hindu University such as we propose, being materialised into being, as also an earnest of the welcome we hope to receive for the deputation that is about to visit Central and Western India. His Highness has proved himself already to be possessed of great public spirit. He has served his King in the Council and in the Field and is always in the front rank of those whose patriotism prompts them to lend a helping hand in all those measures which have for their object the prosperity and the uplifting of the people in India. Before sitting down may I be permitted to say a few words.

2. Your Highness and Gentlemen,——We are met this afternoon as, you are all aware, to promote the scheme for the establishment of a Hindu University for the whole of India. At the Conference which was recently held in Benares, it was agreed that Mrs. Besant, Pundit Mohan Malaviya and myself should co-operate heartily together to bring our cherished project to fruition. We resolved to do nothing without the express sanction and approval of the Government of India. The Government have approved of the erection of a Hindu University and it is along the lines which they have indicated that we are now proceeding and venture to hope that success will ultimately crown our efforts backed, as we know they will be, by the sympathetic co-operation of the enlightened opinion of all the various sections of our community.

3. The noble and inspiring reply of the King-Emperor to the University Deputation on Saturday, 6th January last, ought to send a thrill of hope through the breasts of every educationist in the land. I make no apology for quoting His Majesty's words. He said. "It is to the Universities of India that I look to assist in that gradual union and fusion of the culture and aspirations of Europeans and Indians on which the future well-being of India so greatly depends." And again, "you have to conserve the ancient learning and simultaneously to push forward Western Science. You have also to build up character without which learning is of little value." These words of wisdom surely ring out the death-knell of a godless education, for character can only be built up in so far as it is deeply rooted in the religious life.

4. In another paragraph of his reply, the King-Emperor said. "To-day in India I give to India the watchword of Hope. On every side I trace the signs and strivings of new life. Education has given you hope, and through better and higher education, you will build up higher and better hopes." With these words ringing in our ears we cannot do otherwise than press forward with enthusiasm to the realisation of our scheme for a Hindu University for India.

5. The question of funds is a problem which we will have to solve. We have already received subscriptions amounting to Rs. 40 43 lakhs, which mark a beginning; and which I trust will prove but the earnest of the three crores which, at the least, will be required before a thoroughly equipped University can claim to be of the same rank as those in Europe. But I believe that with enthusiasm through all the ranks of our community in India, condensed into fruitful channels of liberality, the money will not be wanting in due time for the fulfilment of our wishes, and for landing the proposed University into the realm of achievement.

6. We cannot expect that our great project can be fully realised all at once, or indeed probably for a considerable time to come. But we can lay down the broad and definite lines along which we are to proceed with our scheme under the sanction of Government approval, and, making the Central Hindu College at Benares our nucleus, we will from that central heart develop the idea of the University in a natural manner by steps slow but sure, consolidating every important stage as we go along until at last we shall behold before our eyes a Hindu University for India second to none in its equipment for turning out its students into Hindu gentlemen thoroughly grounded in the true principles of religion, good and loyal citizens, able to play their part in public affairs, and cultured in those arts and sciences suitable for their respective callings in life. This surely is a high and noble aim, and one which ought to evoke the enthusiasm and sympathy of our entire community throughout the whole of India.

7. The work of a University, as I take it, is for the development of a student into his true manhood—to make him an all-round good man, giving him the free and disciplined use of all the powers of his tripartite nature, spirit, soul and body, in order that he may take his fitting place in the social order whether in the realm of religion, of law, of medicine, of Arts and Literature, of Commerce or of Music and the Fine Arts, and not least, of Agriculture, which is now and for a long time to come, will be the first and most important interest in the Empire.

8. I need hardly emphasise the fact that first and foremost our Hindu University, to be of any avail, must be penetrated with a truly religious atmosphere. The atmosphere in which it lives and moves and has its being must be spiritual, out and out; an atmosphere in which the students shall live and breathe while pursuing all their secular studies. I think it was Emerson who said to the students in

America. "Young men, keep your eye on the Eternal, and this will exalt the whole of your intellectual life." Never was a truer word spoken, and I trust the students at our Hindu University will take this wise counsel to heart. We hear a great deal spoken about the teaching of morality, and certainly this kind of teaching is better than none. But mere morality, unless rooted and grounded in the principles of true religion, is nothing more than a thin veneer of surface polish possessing no enduring life. It is when the things of the spirit are neglected that individuals and nations decline in power and influence. The great nations which have come and gone largely owe their decay to the fact that when material wealth and all that made for luxury and ease and sensuous indulgence in sport and other pleasure, swamped and put into abeyance and neglect those intellectual and spiritual motives which constitute the real wealth of individuals and National Manhood. India suffers to-day from the same neglect. And it is in order to rouse our Countrymen from their slumber in regard to those higher things which lead on to national greatness and influence of the truest order, that we Hindus propose with heart and soul, as our Mahomedan brethren are doing with such signal service in regard to their community, to provide amongst our people of all classes, from the lowest to the highest ranks in society, an education firmly rooted in the principles of true religion, having love to God and to our fellow-men as the basilar foundation of all our work.

9. Gentlemen, it was inevitable that our scheme should be subjected to criticism in certain quarters, and it is only right that we should welcome criticism when it is of the sane and honest kind. The vast majority of our critics have been sympathetic in their approval of the establishment of a Hindu University, while indicating their own views as to the particular methods of carrying out the scheme. We are glad to have criticism of the constructive order. Such is a real help when endeavouring to work out the details of the constitution. There has also been some criticism of a destructive and rather vitriolic character. This is perhaps only natural, and it arises largely from a deficient perspective. But when time allows of our aims being seen through a dry and clear light, our critics may be expected to see more eye to eye with us in the great purpose we have in view.

10. Our Hindu University will necessarily be a Denominational one. But it will be as remote as the poles from being sectarian. Indeed the atmosphere of a University is one in which a Sectarian spirit cannot live. It is only right that our students should be brought up in the religion of their forefathers, and the more they are grounded in the principles of their own religion, the more broad-minded and sympathetic they become towards those who adhere to other fores. This remarkable feature in the relations which subsist between the followers of the great religions of the world is one for which we should be profoundly thankful. We generally find much bitterness amongst ecclesiastical sectarians within our religion, whose difference of opinion or belief is based upon

some trifling point of interpretation of scripture, but the attitude of
the mass of the followers of our religion towards those of another
is always almost one of toleration and respect. And this is inevi-
tably so, because a man who loves and cherishes the religion of his
forefathers is a religious man all the world over, no matter what
may be his religious creed. The goal is a common one, namely,
spiritual aspiration and the increasing desire for the knowledge of
God. This is the goal towards which Mahomedans and Hindus
alike are now tending in their desire to provide a religious basis for
the education of their children.

11. The Fundamental mistake which our critics make is in
confusing sectarianism with denominationalism. The history of
Religion shows that while ecclesiastics of all creeds fight and squab-
ble amongst themselves, sainthood is one and the same all the world
over and in all religions.

12. We rejoice to think that our Mahomedan countrymen are
similarly engaged in promoting a Mahomedan University at Aligarh, the seat of Mahomedan learning, under the leadership of my
friend H. H. The Agha Khan, and we wish them all success in their
enterprise. They, too, believe with ourselves that only as the intellectual is penetrated with spiritual life, so only can their youths be
fitted to take their true place in the social and political realm as
men of wide culture and true patriotism.

13. The practical and effective answer to the suggestion that
these so-called sectarian institutions will tend necessarily to em-
bitter the feelings between us Hindus and our Mahomedan brethren
lies in the fact of the generous subscriptions I have been offered
from H. H. the Aga Khan, the Raja of Jehangirabad and Mr. Justice Rahim, Mr. Hasan Imam and others, and in the most cordial
messages that have accompanied such gifts. These feelings have
been reciprocated by Hindus—prominent amongst whom have been
H. H. the Maharaja of Gwalior—towards our Mahomedan friends,
and these kindly cordialities surely ought to be looked upon as the
pledges and earnests of a sincere relationship between us and our
Mahomedan friends, and is at the same time a tribute to that unification of spirit which the atmosphere of University life carries with
it wherever it is to be found. The Government of India, in their
cordial approval of the schemes for Mahomedan and Hindu Universities, know full well the unifying effect of such institutions in
the promotion of kindly feelings, and they also know that Universities and University life are valuable assets on the side of loyalty
to law and to the social order. They create goodwill all round and
an atmosphere of life in which deeds of darkness find no place, but
where everything that tends to the uplifting of the people to a higher
platform of being finds sustenance and support.

14. As I have already said our University scheme will necessarily be one of slow growth and development. It will take time to
construct its constitution so as to harmonise all the different views

133

of the numerous sections in which Hinduism finds itself to-day. But time and patience will overcome all difficulties, even the difficulty of obtaining the necessary funds. Of one thing we were certain and that is the Government approval of our scheme and the cordial support of the Education Minister without which we might labour in vain.

15. Gentlemen, I need not detain you further at the present time, as I will have other opportunities of speaking upon this topic. I would, however, refer you to the illuminating pamphlet on "The Hindu University of Benares," by my friend Pundit Madan Mohan Malaviya, which contains a mine of information on the subject, and is worthy of study by all interested in Hindu University Education. I hope and trust that the scheme on which we have embarked will be taken up with enthusiasm, by every Hindu who has the moral regeneration and the intellectual uplift of his people at heart—an enthusiasm which nothing will be allowed to damp until the object of our ardent desire is fully accomplished. Then shall India begin to take her true place amongst the Nations of the world. God speed the day.

Appendix-6

DEPARTMENT OF EDUCATION,
27th February 1912.
19

PRIVATE.

My dear Maharaja,

I knew Durbhunga had that proposal in mind, and advised
him to consult Your Highness about it and, if you did not
agree, as I thought you probably might not, to leave the
patronship open for the present. It is not altogether
desirable that you should publish Mysore's refusal. And
although the terms of his letter preclude a further reference to him now, later on there may be means of inducing
him to change his mind. At any rate it is well to leave
things open.

We are very busy in Council these days. The Dacca
University agitation is dead and after the collapse of the
debate in the Lords we shall hear less of the wickedness
and folly of the move to Delhi.

With kind regards,

Yours very sincerely,

Harcourt, Butler.

FROM

The HON'BLE RAI BAHADUR Dr. SUNDAR LAL, c.i.e.,

SECRETARY, HINDU UNIVERSITY SOCIETY,

ALLAHABAD.

To

His Hi̇̇̇̇̇̇

Lucknow.

No. 4259   Dated, Allahabad, the 19th July 1912.

My dear Maharaja Sahib,

I am glad to acknowledge the receipt of your reply dated 17th July 1912 and with it of the report on the proceedings of the meeting held in Kashmir and of the list of the donations given. The report is interesting reading and is a valuable contribution to the literature of the Hindu University movement. My office has made copies both of the report and of the list and they are, in accordance with your desire, returned to you.

I hope to see some mention of the work done by your Highness in connection with the Hindu University movement in the report, I am expecting from the Hon'ble Pandit Madan Mohan Malaviya. The hints given of your independent activity are additional points and they will of course find a place in the six-monthly report.

I am,

Yours sincerely,

Appendix-9

--------*--------

Yesterday (July the first) must be regarded as one of
the most memorable days in the history of modern Kashmir. For
it was yesterday that witnessed a great and noble act perform-
-ed by its ruler who was joined in it's loyalty and in full
and hearty co-operation by all his subjects and servants, Hindu
and Mussalman even though the act performed concerned chiefly
the Hindu Community of which His Highness the Maharaja Sahib
Bahadur of Kashmir is both an ornament and one of the principal
leaders. This act consisted in His Highness' making an
announcement, in a great public meeting and in response to a
touching appeal made by the Hon'ble the Maharaja Sahib
Bahadur of Dharbhanga, of His Highness' contribution to the
Hindu University movement which has now for over two years
been so powerfully moving the Hindu Community in all its
sections in all parts of the country. The deed and the
occasion were unique not only for the noble gift which His
Highness the Maharaja Sahib made to the Hindu University
but for the spirit by which the whole of the proceedings were
animated and all present were dominated. For it was a spirit
of love and brotherliness, not only among the Hindus present
but between these on the one hand and the Muhamedan subjects
and servants of His Highness as a body on the other, and a
spirit of united loyalty and devotion on the part of both
the Communities to the throne and person of His Gracious
and Imperial Majesty the King and Emperor, as representing
the Divine Ruling Power, the Raja-Shakti, among us—a loyalty
and devotion which, while both the donor and the princely
mendicant and receiver are pre-eminently noted for its
possession, has been characterised by a Viceroy himself as

137

ever unflinching on the part of His Highness the Maharaja
Sahib Bahadur of Kashmir.It is this spirit of loving brother-
-liness between the representatives of the two great Communities of India on the one hand and of their united loyalty
and devotion to the Divine Ruling Power now manifest through
the British, which may be safely described as the leading
feature of the proceedings of yesterday which gave it such
a noble character, apart from the nobility of the gift which
was but an indication and an earnest of what might still be
expected from His Highness as was declared by His Chief
Minister on His Highness' behalf.Let us hope and pray that
this spirit may dominate the fresh life that the Hindu
University is to pour into the almost lifeless body politic
of the Hindu Community while it fosters its growth anew as
a solidly united and strongly individual organism.May there
be no bitterness of hostility to any other Community in the
newly invigorating sap of life and no counterflow to that
larger and stronger current which issuing forth from the
life Divine finds an imperial expression in the King and
Emperor.

Truly was the day and occasion a most memorable one
which saw the manifestation of this spirit in Kashmir as it
did at the public meeting held yesterday at the Hazuri Bagh
in Srinagar in connection with the Hindu University movement
in the interest of which the Hon'ble the Maharaja Sahib
Bahadur of Dharbhanga had been visiting Kashmir.

The meeting had been announced at 4 p.m. under the
Presidency of His Highness the Maharaja Sahib Bahadur of
Kashmir with the Maharaja Sahib,Bahadur of Dharbhanga as the
principal speaker.And although it had to be postponed till
5.30 p.m. the grounds of the Hazuri Bagh already presented a

picturesque and animated ⌃ of moving crowds by the time the
clock struck four till there gathered together a vast concourse
of people numbering some ten thousands when the proceedings
began on the arrival of His Highness the Maharaja Sahib
Bahadur at the appointed hour. The Maharaja Bahadur of Dharbhanga had arrived a few minutes earlier and received His
Highness the ~~appointed~~ President of the meeting on his arrival.
The business of the day at once began according to a pre-
arranged programme. And immediately on the music which had
been going on having ceased two students from the local Sri
Paratap College chanted the well known Kashmiri Manglacharna in
Sanskrit.
        This was followed by the recitation of Sanskrit verses &
composed for the occasion by Pandits Nityananda Shastri and
Janardan of Kashmir and also by Brahmachari Brahmanand. The
young and greatly promising son of Pandit Din Dayal, the
famous and gifted Hindu speaker, read out a well written
speech in Sanskrit--his maiden speech we were told-- setting
forth the objects and need of the proposed Hindu University
and showing how such a scheme was not entirely unprecedented
among the Hindus, they having had Universities of their own
in the ancient days in Nalanda, Taksha-Shila and other places.
        Lala Lakshmi Das also made a short speech and read a
Hindi poem eulogising the services of the principal workers
in the cause and expressing gratefulness to them on behalf
of the Hindu Community.
        He was followed by Pandit Jagadish Chandra Chatterji
who by command of His Highness the President and in obedience
to the wishes of the Maharaja Sahib Bahadur of Dharbhanga,
                    ⌃ in a few words
explained ⌃ in English the good the Hindu University movement
was and would be doing to the community and to the nation
apart from the purely educational benefits which would of

139

course follow.He showed how the movement was the first and
only one which had powerfully struck the imagination of,and
stirred to the innermost depths,the whole of the Hindu
Community,how it was already bringing together in warm co-ope-
-ration the Hindus of all sections all over the country and
was making of them a united whole and how this alone was
worth spending crores of Rupees on,apart from all other
considerations;how this spirit of unification and co-operation
was not producing,and should not produce ,any spirit of
hostility towards the sister community of our Muhamedan
brethren who were also working for a University of their own,
moved by the same spirit as the Hindus but was and should be
drawing the two communities together,each growing in its own
line as a strongly individual body but with warm and brother-
ly feelings towards the other,and how finally the two communi
-ties,thus joining hands each with the other should never
lose sight of their duty to the Sovereign Ruling Power,being
ever loyal and devoted to it as a manifestation of the Divine
Power.

Mr.Chatterji was followed by Lala Jiwan Mal Kakkar,
Rais of Peshawar who in a speech in Urdu explained how in the
olden days India was prosperous in every respect and how and
for what reason her fall was brought about,how the country
needed more knowledge and therefore more Universities indeed
having a
which the population far outnumbered that of other countries
where there were a much larger number of Universities than in
India and how the proposed Hindu University was a great
desideratum.

Then spoke Pandit Gopinath Sahib,Private Secretary
to the Maharaja Sahib Bahadur of Dharbhanga and a member of
the Deputation,who in an eloquent speech in Hindi explained

further the same idea showing how the spirit of friendly
co-operation between the two Communities found a noble
expression in the gifts which His Highness Sir Aga Khan and
the Maharaja Sahib Bahadur of Dharbhanga made respectively
to the Hindu and Muhamedan Universities.He also explained
how this being the age of war not so much with arms as
with knowledge,the Hindu University,as the Muhamedan Universi
-ty was needed.

The next speaker was the famous Hindi orator Pandit
Din Dayal who in charming language which is all his own
showed how the proposed University was to revive the ancient
learning of the land again and how not only the Maharajas
of Kashmir and Mithila,the one representing the ancient
Surya Vamsha and the other the Brahmins and Rishis of the
past were that day gathered together in noble co-operation
to further the cause of the University but how these were also
the learned Rishis of the past themselves,Vyasa,Valmiki,Kanada
Patanjali,present there in spirit if we had only eyes to see;
and how each,overjoyed at the prospect of the learning of
which he was the promugator in the past being revived,was
holding forth his contribution of knowledge to the University
that was to be and was blessing it with their thoughts and
prayers.The Pandit's comparison of the present occasion to
the celebrated Episode in the Ramayana when Vishvamitra came
to Dasharatha to beg from him the services of his son for the
cause of righeousness was very telling.

Deeply moved as the assembly was by the spontaneous
persuasive eloquence of Pandit Din Dayal,it had now the
privilege of listening to the touching appeal which the
Maharaja Bahadur of Dharbhanga addressed in Hindi to His
Highness of Kashmir,His Chief Minister,the other ministers

and servants of His Highness and to the general public. The
Maharaja Bahadur speaking in Hindi said in purport as follows:-

"It is a matter of great delight to me that today we
have for the President of this vast meeting my noble friend,
His Highness the Maharaja Sahib Bahadur of Kashmir whose free
presence adds so much to the glory of the gathering. It is also
a matter of pleasure to me to think how we have met together
in this beautiful land which was held consecrated owing to
the presence in it of Rishis and Tapasvin and which had a
great reputation for learning in the past so as to merit the
appelation of Sharada Pitha,-- and met for a purpose which
pertains at once both to piety and learning.

Now-a-days the education we are having is devoid of
religious teaching, and the consequence is that it is under-
mining almost all that is noblest and best in us -- in both
Hindus and Muhamedans. And with the loss of religion and noble
ideas there is bitterness of feeling and conflict between
these two great Communities of the country -- far more so
than it would be the case fifty years ago. If a man has no
respect for what is of a pious character in his own religion he
can scarcely have it for similar ideas in others.

But the Government can scarcely be blamed for this
result. For the Government is neither Hindu nor Mussalman and
could hardly be expected to teach the religion of either. They
have therefore been satisfied with imparting a purely secular
education with the result mentioned above.

It has therefore been felt a necessity by the Hindu
and Mussalman leaders of the country, that the country be
provided with two Denominational Universities for imparting
education with religion to the youngmen of the two Communities.

And it is incumbent on Hindu nobles and States to

render as much help to the proposed University as has been
rendered by the Muhammadan States and nobles to the cause of
the Muhamedan University.

I am a Brahmin and it has been the practice of the
Brahmins of old to beg.And although I have not been personally
in the habit of begging before,I still come before you in the
capacity of a mendicant and I hope and trust that you will
give with your whole heart and soul, so that I may be encourag-
-ed in my new profession, and that I may not go away empty-
handed to be laughed at by the public.I am sure can assure you I am a
mendicant whose heart is weighed down with the anxious thoughts
and cares for the success of the proposed University, but for
which there is scarcely hope for the regeneration of the
Hindus as a nation.

Your Highness,you are an ornament to the Kshatriya
race,belonging to the noble Solar family and your piety is
known fully far and wide,you are like a veritable Rajarshi,
knowing the full duties of a king;--I appeal unto you.

And you the Chief Minister of His Highness,you are
born in the noble family of the Diwans of Kashmir.

And you His Highness' other Ministers,servants and
nobles and subjects--I appeal unto you also.

I have come to you all as a mendicant in the interest
of this great religious cause and you have treated me well
for which I thank you heartily.I beg from you such gifts for
the Hindu University as will ensure the success of the movement,will render my efforts fruitful and will add lustre to the
name,be and to the glory of the Kashmir State,the Kashmir Maharaja
his ministers and subjects and all.May God bless you all."

To this appeal His Highness the Maharaja Sahib
Bahadur of Kashmir replied in noble and eloquent words which

was visibly animated by a spirit which was full of love for the ideals of Hinduism and of a sincere and genuine desire for the welfare of the Hindu Community as it was characterised by by a noble and impartial love for his subjects irrespective of religious difference and by a noble and exalted loyalty and devotion to the throne and person of His Imperial Majesty the King and Emperor.His Highness said as follows:---

" Maharaja Sahib of Dharbhanga who is an old friend of mine is here in connection with the Hindu University movement.I am sorry his stay is going to be very short.He has, you will be glad to learn,been gazetted as a member of the Executive Council of Behar.We should be grateful to the Imperial Government for having conferred this honour upon one who is the leader of the Hindu Community as represented by the Dharma Maha Mandala.It is a happy sign--which be-tokens marvellous progress that has been made-- that it has become possible for Raisis to meet together.In olden times, the Raisis could not meet.They could not join even socially one with the other.Under the Pax-Britaica which rules supreme,the old world suspicions no longer pervail.The facili--ties for intercourse made it possible for me to have Social relations with my Rajput brothers in other parts of the country.This is but one of the blessings of the British Government which are manifold and it is possible for every one to pursue his lawful occupations without molestation.

I just referred to Maharaja Dharbhanga's appoint-ment as a member of the Executive Council of Behar.I trust his appointment will not in any way interfere with the mission which he has so much at heart.I have every hope that the Maharaja will take permission of the Government of India to see his life-work fulfilled and steer the ship clear of the shoals and pitfalls--for there is no one else who wields so great an influence with the aristocracy and the middle classes which the Maharaja wields alike by his wealth,educa-

144

the movement should have been started under so high auspices.
It is still more fortunate that at this time we have an
Education Member in Sir H.Butler whose valuable advice and
guidance we cannot too adequately give praise.Sir H.Butler
will,I am sure,instil a spirit in the movement which will
make the University shine all the more and shed its lustre
upon all who will be privileged to profit by it.

We have,moreover,at this time a Viceroy whose
consumonate statesmanship and varied experience is an asset.
The valuable advice of His Excellency the Viceroy will
certainly make the Universities,both Hindu and Muhamedan,
ideal ones.

I am happy that my subjects both Hindu and Muhamedan
have mustered so strong to day.Their appearing together to
further the cause which this movement has in view establishes that they are one in sympathy and ideals.

In the anxious times through which British India
lately passed and which are now happily over,thanks to the
wise statesmanship of the Powers that be, not a speck of a
cloud of lawlessness was visible in my territories and I
attribute this to the brotherliness of the two Communities
and to their ingrained loyalty which they have,as my subjects
for the British crown.

The contributions that my subjects make must be
entirely voluntary--there is no compulsion of any kind.Every
one is expected to contribute his mite according to his
capacity.

My Chief Minister Rai Sahib Diwan Amar Nath C.I.E.
will just announce my donation which the State will give.
The University will,I have a firm faith in the wisdom of its
organisers make a fundamental and cardinal principle of its

constitution that worship of the Almighty Lord and loyalty
to the British Government will be its two corner-stones. The
alumni of the University will I hope turn out to be men of
cultured hearts--who will not despoil the sacred knowledge
imparted to them, who will not abuse the Power which knowledge
confers. Who will, as matter of principle, bring the blessings
of education within the reach of every one, who will be fired
by the ambition of making the name Hindu synonymous with a
loyal and devoted heart and useful citizenship."

His Highness was followed by his Chief Minister who,
by command, announced the gift of His Highness in the following words:--

"His Highness the Maharaja Sahib Bahadur has comman
-ed me to announce on his behalf that he very generously
grants for ever from the State Treasury Rs1000/- a month (i.e
Rs12000/- a year) as an aid to the Hindu University. This is
an evident proof that His Highness has a heart-felt sympathy
with the aims and objects of the Hindu University wherein
the educational progress and prosperity of the Hindu nation
will greatly depend.

While announcing this I consider it proper and
necessary to state that as I take it the objects of the
Hindu University would be not only to give a literary education
but also to establish technical institutions whereby the cause
of useful arts and industries would be furthered to the benefit
of the public. Thus only would the Hindu University be able to
meet the requirements of the present age.

His Highness has further ordered me to declare
that he will constantly bear in mind the needs of the Hindu
University as it advances on practical lines and would make
occasional grants and donations in future as well."

This announcement, which really means, apart from
promises of future donations, a present gift of Rs3,50,000/-
~~~~~~~~ being the capitalised value of the annual grant of
Rs12000/- was received with great cheers and the Maharaja
Bahadur of Dharbhanga acknowledged it with thanks.

Then came an appeal to the officials and Raises of
the State and the general public, again by Pandit Din Dayal
speaking on behalf of the Maharaja Bahadur of Dharbhanga.
And in response, there came promises and announcements from
all sides of the gathering, the Muhammadans vying with the Hindus
in their alacrity to contribute.

Of these gifts, one of Rs5000/- was promised on
behalf of Raj Kumar Shri Hari Singh Sahib and Rs2000/- on
that of Maharaj Kumar Jagatdev Singh, the adopted son of His
Highness the Maharaja Sahib Bahadur.

The gift of the Chief Minister Rai Sahib Diwan Amar
Nath Sahib C.I.E. was in the form of an annual grant to the
University of Rs1200/- i.e. Rs100/- a month from his Estate.
Of this amount Rs1000/- is to be regarded as coming from
himself and Rs200/- from his son, Diwan Dr.Badri Nath, the
Private Secretary to His Highness of Kashmir. The announcement
of the gift was also of Diwan Amar Nath was also received
enthusiastically as the gathering realised that it really
meant in capital value a gift of about Rs 30,000/- at 3½ per cent.
per annum.

The gifts of the three Ministers---the Home Minister,
Rai Bahadur Dr. A.Mitra, the Judicial Minister, Rai Bahadur
Pandit Radha Kishen Kaul and the Revenue Minister, Sheikh
Makbul Hussain ammounted to Rs500/- each.

While the other donations announced on the spot were
as follows:-

LIST OF DONORS OF THE HINDU UNIVERSITY.

---------*---------

amount.

1. Lala Shiv Das, Chief Judge, Kashmir.   250/-

2. Choudhri Khushi Mohammad, Governor,
   Kashmir.   100/-

3. General Bhag Singh Officer
   Commanding, Kashmir Division.   100/-

4. R.B.Col.Diwan Bishen Das.   250/-

5. Bhai Dan Singh, Secretary to Chief
   Minister.   200/-

6. Pandit Udey Chand, Secretary to H.H.   200/-

7. Col.Samandar Khan, Adjutant General.   50/-

8. Col.Anant Ram, Quarter Master General.   100/-

9. Maulvi Nazir Ahmed, Judge Small Cause
   Court.   20/-

10. Pandit Parduman Kishen, Sub-Judge Ist.
    grade.   100/-

11. R.S.Sardar Ganda Singh D.EN.Kashmir.   200/-

12. Pandit J.C.Chatterji, Director Archaeology.   100/-

13. L.Jagat Ram, Asstt.Secretary to C.M.   50/-

14. Bakhshi Sardar Singh Offg.Vernacular
    Secretary to H.H.   25/-

15. Mr.R.D.Pande, Secretary to Education
    Minister.   100/-

16. Wazir Sobha Ram, General Treasurer.   500/-

17. Sardar Mul Singh Khosla.P.A. to H.M.   25/-

18. L.Shanker Lal P.A. to Home Minister.   50/-

19. Malik Sher Mohammad P.A. to R.M.   15/-

20. Diwan Bansi Lal P.A. to Settlement
    Commissioner.   50/-

21. ....it Suraj Ram Mattu, Treasury Officer.   5..

22. ..L.Gobin.... Asstt.Acco..
    General.

23. L.Dyal Chand, Chief Supdt. Acc......   75/-
    General's office.

24. Pandit Daulat Ram, Examiner Local Acc......   50/-

25. Lala Ram Sarn, Inspector Police.   15/-

26. L.Lal Chand, Deputy Inspector do.   10/-

27. Mehta Kirpa Ram, tutor to the Maharaj   10/-
    Kumar.

28.Diwan Brij Lal,Tahsildar Srinagar.   25/-

29.Bawa Balvant Singh,Inspecor of Schools.   25/-

30.Pandit Anant Ram,Supdt. Toshakhana.   50/-

31.Pandit Kirpa Ram,Sopdt.Dharmarth.   50/-

32.Wazir Para Ram,Supdt.Police,Kashmir.   200/-

33.Wazir Din Dayal,Tahvildar Toshakhana.   100/-

34.Pandit Deo Kak Muneiff.   50/-

35.Lala Sukh Dayal Sawhney,Sub.Judge 2nd grade.   50/-

36.Pandit Kishen Lal Muneiff.   25/-

37.Diwan Anant Ram Aswal B.A.,L.L.B.   100/-

38.Diwan Shib Saran   500/-

39.Pandit Vish Ram,Manager Kashmir State
   property Bhadarwah Jagir.   100/-

40.Mr.L.C.Bose,Electrical Engineer.   50/-

41.L.Niranjan Das,Head Master,State High School.   20/-

42.L.Shiv Chand M.A. Professor Hindu College.   51/-

43.Pandit Gyani Ram B.A.   do   do   51/-

44.Lala Parshotam Ram,Hazirbash.   50/-

45.Col.Ishri Singh,Asstt.Adjutant General.   25/0

46.Major Bharat Singh.   15/-

47.Major Diwan Chet Ram,Deputy Asstt.Quarter
   Master General.   15/-

48.Major Isher Das,Supdt.C-in-C's office.   25/-

49.Sardar Gopal Singh S.D.O.   25/-

50.Lala Anant Sarup c/o of late Rai Jora Mal.   5/-

51.Hakim Syed Hussain W.W.Udhampur.   25/-

53.Babu Hari Chand, Generall's office,srah.   25/-

54.Pandit Kashi Ram,Supdt.   15/-

55.Pandit Inder Kishen,Accountant Foreign office.   15/-

56.L.Sarni Mal,member Samatan Dharm Sabha,Kashmir office.25/-

57.L.Tara Chand Hakim Chief Minister and his son.   25/-

58.Bakhshi Gokal Chand,Governor's office.   25/-

                                                                       15/-

59.Lala Balmakund,Accountant General's office.   10/-

60.Pandit Rajkishen,Sub-overseer.   10/-

61.Pandit Karm Chand,Agricultural Deptt.   5/-

62.Pandit Tara Chand,Tahsildar,Uri.cash.   15/-

63.L.Samlubhaya,Supdt.Revenue Minister office.   15/-

64.Pandit Sahib Mahadeo Rai,cash.   1/-

65.4 friends.A.B.C.D. through B.M.Verma,local a/cs.   30/-

66.Khwaja Samadju Kakru   100/-

67.Sardar Ganda Singh,Maharajganj.   125/-

68.Pandit Vidh Lal Dhar,Rais of Kashmir.   250/-

69.Rai Gobind Ram's sons.   15/-

70.Messrs.N.D.Hari Ram & Brothers.   500/-

71.Pandit Bisheshar Nath Razdan.   50/-

72.Sardar Hakim Singh Contractor.   500/-

73.Pandit Rishib Ram Contractor.   500/-

74.Pandit Isherjoo   25/-

75.Thakur Ram Chand of Peshawar.   100/-

76.Rai Bahadur Ram Saran Das,Rais of Lahore.   1000/-

77.Mir Waiz,Kashmir.   25/-

78.Akbar Shah   12/-

79.Mian Wali Shah   5/-

80.Khwaja Hussan Shah   6/-

81.Pandit Hargopal Vakil   20/-

82.Messrs.Jawahir Lal and Sons.   125/-

84.Pakhani A/c.Ram Pleader,cash.   10/-

85.L.Malawa Ram,Supdt. Agriculture's pivate.   25/-

86.Babu Isher Das,Supdt.Judge High Court's office.   10/-

87.Pandit Vish Nath Photographer.   25/-

88.Pandit Din Dayal   50/-

89.R.B.Girdhari Lal Mir Munshi to H.H. the Lieutenant Governor of the Punjab.   200/-

    100/-

90. Lala Shanker Das Isher Das,Maharajganj. 25/-

91. Dr.Dayal Das,Asstt.Surgeon, do . 25/-

92. Lala Tara Chand incharge Director Agriculture. 15/-

93. L.Ram Kishen Newspaper Reader to His Highness. 10/-

94. Lala Devi Dayal Lodi Ram,Maharajganj. 10/-

95. Lala Radhakishen Mohan Singh, do 15/-

96. Lala Sobha Ram Shaker Das, do 10/-

97. Pandit Hari Ram   do 15/-

98. Maharaja Sahib's Cricket team. 25/-

99. Pandit Autar Kishen Professor Hindu College. 51/-

100. Sultan Mutwali Khan Jagirdar Kathai 250/-

101. Babu Charanjit lala Manager Bharat Bank,Srinagar.10/-

102. Mr.C.J.Burrow,State Band Master. 10/-

103. Thakur Raghunath Singh,Asstt.Supdt. stables. 10/-

104. Pandit Sona Dar Vakil 20/-

105. Pandit Nityanand Shastri 5/-

106. Lala Karam Chand of Bmnabad. 10/-

107. Pandit Jia Lal Dhar .50/-

108. Bhagat Khazana Mal Goor Das, Maharajganj. 50/-

109. Sukh Dayal Amar Chand 50/-

110. Lala Fateh Chand Deputy Inspector Customs & Excise.10/

111. Seth Phattu (H.H.'s private Deptt.) 200/-

112. Thakur Raghunath Singh do 25/-

113. Pandit Mani Ram do 15/-

114. Pandit Tara Mani cash do 50/-

115. Lala Har Bhagwan Das do 15/-

116. Lala Shiv Nath do 25/-

117. Pandit Vishva Nath Pujari do 50/-

118. L. S. Sharma. do 20/-

These announcements made two Committees were formed
--one for Srinagar and the other for Jammu for the collection
of the promised donations and subscriptions and for getting
new ones.

16.

Throughout the meeting great Enthusiasm prevailed which it was most elevating to behold. By the time the proceedings came to an end it had already grown dark and lamps had to be lighted when at about 9 p.m. the meeting dispersed with a vote of thanks to the chair and cheers for the King-Emperor, for His Highness the President and for the Maharaja Bahadur of Dharbhanga.

Appendix-10

Reply of H. H. The Msharaja of Darbhanga, to an address delivered by the Members of the Pradhan Bhumihar Brahman Sabha, to His Highness at Bankipore on 28th July 1912.

GENTLEMEN,—Members of the Pradhan Bhumihar Brahman Sabha. I have to thank you for the kind and all too flattering address you have just presented to me and especially for the spirit which pervades it.

I accept your congratulations in a very thankful manner on my appointment as an Executive Member of the Council of the New Province, and beg to assure you that I prize very highly indeed the honour which the Government have conferred upon me in placing me in such a position of trust and responsibility in connection with the Government of Bihar and Orissa.

I accepted the appointment not merely as a personal honour, much as I also deem it in that light, but in the hope that, as a representative of the people, and knowing their wants and their hopes for the future prosperity of the Province, I may, in my humble way, during my term of office contribute in some small degree, and according to my ability to the fulfilment of your legitimate aspirations.

You have been pleased to refer to my connection with the Bharat Dharma Mahamandal, I assure you that the interests of this great All-India Movement for the revival of Hindu spiritual religion is one that lies very near to my heart and all the best energy and influence I possess will be used for the furtherance of this great

You make reference also in your address to my efforts to promote the erection of a Hindu University for the whole of India. I have just returned from a somewhat comprehensive tour undertaken in the interests of the University, in the course of which I have, as a Member of deputation, visited a number of the larger centres in Upper India and Cashmere, and I have been gratified beyond all expectation at the splendid reception with which the University Scheme has everywhere been received and also at the princely subscriptions which have been given towards its erection. It is our hope that in course of time we will have a noble Hindu University founded on a strictly religious basis, and equipped with all the appointments of a first-rate Institution in professional staff and apparatus, for giving the students a wide general culture as well as fitting them for their individual vocational callings in life.

I do not need to be assured that your Community, as conservative and Hindus, are loyal and law-abiding citizens, and I am sure you may with confidence rely upon the sympathy and encouragement of the Government not only in the important matter of education, but in all others having for their aim the well-being of the people of the Province. But let me tell you as a matter of practical advice and counsel that, according to the old adage, Providence only helps those who are willing to help themselves. You must not expect the Government to do everything for you. You must also do your duty in the matter of self-help if you expect the Government to do theirs.

I have again to thank you for your kind address and for your good wishes for my future life.

Printed at the Beharee Press, Bankipore.

The Palace,
Bhavnagar.

3rd February, 1913.

My dear Maharaja Saheb,

I am glad to receive your letter of the 20th January.
The country owes you a heavy debt of gratitude for your self-
sacrifice and untiring labours in the important cause of the
Hindu University. I note that the Deputation intends visiting
Kathiawad some time in February this year, and it would have
given me great delight to welcome you to my Capital, had it
not been for the fact that I shall be unavoidably absent -
about the time you mention. Moreover I may mention that the
last year's famine fell upon Kathiawad with some severity and
that coupled with other extraordinary expenses have taxed -
our resources a good deal of late. And speaking for myself
I would ask - I beg of you to kindly excuse the frankness -
that much as I appreciate the great cause you have undertaken
I may be permitted to defer the consideration of my donation
to a future and more suitable time. I may add that when the
proper time comes, I shall not stand in need of any persua-

-tion or personal appeal. I trust I will not be misunderstood.
Hoping you are well and with kind regards,

Yours sincerely,

Bhavsinh

MADHO BILAS
·SIPRI·

2nd August 1912.

As promised in Simla I am sending
you for your kind perusal, by Registered
packet Post, a few of the Readers which I had
been able to get ready during the last and the
present year.

These Readers I have prepared in
connection with my Educational Scheme. At
present they are in the draft form and as
soon as they are made perfect I propose to
have them translated in all languages.

There are more to be made yet and
as they get completed, I shall keep them on
sending to you from time to time with your
kind permission.

I shall be extremely grateful if
you be so kind as to favour me with your
creticism on them.

25th December 1912

My dear Friend,

Many thanks for your letter of the 18th Instt in connection with your proposed Visit to Jodhpur. I will be very busy till H. E the Viceroy's Visit to Jodhpur is over. I am sorry under the circumstances I will have to ask you to fix some other date in the latter half of February. It would be convenient to you and me both if the change be made in your programme accordingly, or when I write to you next.

Yours sincerely

B——

Maharaja ——

No: 544.

My Dear Maharaja Sahib,

I regret the delay which has occurred owing to
business in replying to your kind letter of the 18th February last
in which you invite my support of the Hindu University scheme.
Such a cause it is needless to say has my cordial support: but
before deciding as to the exact form my contribution shall take
I should be grateful if you will at your convenience favour me
with information as to the probable date when the scheme will
materialise and will also add such details as will help me to
come to a decision as to which of the alternative forms of
assistance mentioned by you I shall adopt.

With kindest regards,

Believe me,

Yours very Sincerely,

Appendix-12

Dated Darbhanga, the 28th April 1913.

From—The Hon'ble Maharaja Sir Rameshwar Singh Bahadur, K.C.I E.,
of Darbhanga, Bankipur,

To —The Hon'ble Sir Harcourt Butler, K.C.S.I., C.I.E.

I have much pleasure in addressing you on the subject of the Hindu University. I have now obtained detailed information as to my financial position from Rai Bahadur Pandit Sunder Lal.

2. I propose, in the first place, to explain our exact financial position and, in the second place, to suggest for your consideration and advice the steps that we might now take to bring into existence the Hindu University at an early date.

3. As to the financial position, as you are already aware, the subscriptions promised go well over 80 lakhs. We have not yet gone to the great bulk of the Native States throughout India. We have approached only a few of them, and have received liberal responses. I hope in the next winter to pay a visit to Mysore and Southern India. The amount, however, actual received from the subscribers up to date is Rs. 21,37,539-8-11½. Out of this sum the amount in the hands of the Society directly is Rs. 21,08,180-2-5½. The balance of Rs. 29,359-6-6 is in the hands of the Secretaries of local committees or private Banks or persons who have been carrying on the work of collections. The amount of course will be coming into the Allahabad office in the ordinary course. The amount collected have been mainly invested in Government Promissory Notes. We own to-day Government. Promissory Notes of the face value of Rs. 21,59,900, carrying interest at 3½ per cent, and the uninvested amount is being invested in the same way. The capital fund in hand may thus be roughly said to be Rs. 20,80,769 4·6 invested in purchasing Government Promissory Notes and Rs. 84,189-1-2½ in other forms; total Rs. 21,64,958-5-8½, including interest (Rs. 25,063-11-6) and miscellaneous receipts (Rs. 2,355-1-3).

4. Besides this amount the following amounts which have been granted by the Ruling Chiefs have yet to be collected :—

1. His Highness the Maharaja of Gwalior	...	...	5 lakhs.
2. Ditto	ditto	Alwar	...	... 2 ,,
3. Ditto	ditto	Bikaneer	...	... 1 lakh.
4. Ditto	ditto	Nabha	...	... 1 ,,
5. Ditto	ditto	Benares	...	... 1 ,,
6. (Balance of)	ditto	Jodhpur	...	... 1 ,,

Total ... 11 lakhs

5. In addition to this there is a sum of Rs. 3 lakhs on account of the balance of my donation These may be taken almost as paid, as they will be realised as soon as the Government desires that the amounts should be paid in. These amounts total 14 lakhs.

6. In addition to these amounts the Maharaja of Cossimbazar is transferring property in trust of the value of one lakh which would bring Rs. 3,500 a year and Babu Brajendra Kishore Roy Chaudhry, who is also a donor of one lakh, is similarly transferring property which would bring us Rs 3,500 a year more net. In other words, they will not pay the money in cash but propose to give property which will bring an equal amount of net income. I am expecting drafts of the necessary documents from these gentlemen.

7. Besides these I may mention the names of the following donors Rs. 50,000 and above, whose donations I expect tnere will be no difficulty whatsoever in collecting :—

1. Raja Kalanand Singh and the Hon'ble Knwar Krityanand Singh of Raj Banaily	...	...	1 lakh.
2. The Maharani of Hathwa	...	...	1 ,,
3. The Hon'ble Rana Sir Sheo Raj Singh of Khajurgaon, Raibareli	...	...	1¼ lakhs.
4. Seth Narotem Moraji Gokul Das (ex-Sheriff of Bombay)	...		1 lakh.
5. Thakur Suraj Bux Singh, Taluqdar of Kasmanda, Sitapur (out of 1 lakh Rs. 35,000 having been paid).			65,000
6. Raja Kristo Das Law	...	...	75,000
7. Rai Ram Charan Das Bahadur	...	...	75.000
8. Balance still payable out of Rai Bahadur Sunder Lal's donation of one lakh.			25,000
Total	...	...	6,65,000

8. There are of course a very large number of donors of amounts below Rs. 50,000. Thus in Allahabad alone may be mentioned the names of :—

			Rs.
1. Lala Bisheshar Das	...	...	25,000
2. Chaudhry Mahadeo Prasad	...	...	25,000
3. Raja Salib of Manda	...	...	20,000
4. Lalas Shambu Nath Lachhmi Narain		...	20,000

In Lucknow, Rai Prag Narain Bhargava Bahadur has paid Rs. 5,000 out of his donation of Rs. 30,000. His balance of Rs. 25,000 will be paid up in a few days. Raja Ram Pal Singh, who is a donor of Rs. 20,000 has paid Rs. 10,000. The balance of Rs. 10,000 will be paid later on. I need not take into account the vast number of donors of smaller amounts who have paid in part their donations, and from most of whom there will be no difficulty in recovering the balance.

9. Three Ruling Chiefs have granted in perpetuity the payment of the following sums :—

			Rs.
His Highness the Maharaja of Jodhpur	...	...	24,000 a year.
His Highness the Maharaja of Kashmir	...	...	12,000 a year.
His Highness the Maharaja of Bikaner	...	...	12,000 a year.
Total	...	...	48,000 a year.

These allowances when capitalised at the rate of 3½ per cent come to about 14 lakhs in value. There are other persons besides who have promised annual or monthly donations in various amounts.

10. Taking the amounts shown in paragraphs 2 to 8 of this letter the amount of the money in hand which may be safely taken as already in hand may be set forth as below :—

			Rs.
(a) Net amount already in hand, including interest realised	...		21,38,738
(b) Amount to be paid by Ruling Chiefs and the Hon'ble the Maharaja of Darbhanga	...	...	14,00,000
(c) Amount which will be paid in property as per paragraph 3			2,00,000
(d) Amount of donations above Rs. 50,000 as per paragraph 6			6,65,000
(e) Capitalised value of annual grants by the Ruling Chiefs, as per paragraph 8	...	...	14,00,000
Total	...	...	58,03,738

11. The great bulk of the balance I have not taken into account for the purposes of this note, although it includes items like Rs. 10,000 each granted by the two Maharanis of Bikaner and Rs. 5,000 of the Maharaj Kumar, Rs. 5,000 by Raj Kumar Hari Singh Saheb of Jammu and Kashmir, Rs. 1,200 per annum by Rai Sahib Dewan Amar Nath, C.I.E., of Kashmir, Rs. 25,000 by Dewan Daya Kishen Kaul of Alwar, Rs. 10,000 by Pandit Sukhdeo Prasad, C.I.E., retired Minister, Marwar State, Rs. 50,000 of Raj Kumar Harihar Prasad of Amawan, Rs. 20,000 of Babu Kamta Shiromni Prasad Singh, Taluqdar of Sehipur, Fyzabad, Rs. 15,000 of Thakurain Sriram Koer, Taluqdar of Khapradih and Rs. 5,000 of Srimati Janki Bai of Bithoor, all in landed property; Rs. 15,000 of Thakur Ganga Bux Singh of Tikari, Rai Bareli, balance of Rs. 15,000 of Raja Chandra Sekhar of Sissendy and Rs. 10,000 of Raja Lalta Prasad of Pilibhit. Rs. 15,000 each of Raja Udai Raj Singh of Kashipur and the Hon'ble Raja Kushal Pal Singh of Kotla.

12. We have not taken into consideration the value of the Central Hindu College which if I remember aright the Hon'ble Mr. Sharp put down at about 14 lakhs. The amount which the Hon'ble Mr. Sharp thought will be required was between Rs. 40,00,000 lakhs and Rs. 50,00,000 lakhs. I think, taking into consideration the amount mentioned in paragraph 9, which may be taken to be as realised for all practical purposes, we have raised more than the amount required, and I think we are now in a position to ask the Government to be so good as to take into consideration the legislation necessary for bringing the University into existence. We have thus financially made out a good case, and if the work proceed as it has been going on till now we shall be able to collect a much larger amount.

13. You were pleased to communicate to the Hon'ble the Raja of Mahmudabad intimation of the fact that the Government had granted one lakh a year recurring to the Muslim University. This was in addition to the large amount that the Government was already paying to the M. A. O. College, Aligarh, and which of course would be continued on its incorporation with the Muslim University. The cost of the necessary buildings and apparatus for the setting up of a first-class University is very heavy. The figures recently prepared for the Dacca University Scheme give an idea of the amount required. It is now evident that by reason of the curtailment of the scope of the University we cannot get any large amount from Bengal or the Punjab, nor from Madras or Bombay. The Central Provinces as well as the new province of Behar and Orissa are each looking forward to the establishment of their own Provincial Universities. Our situation has thus become much more difficult by reason of the curtailment of the scope of our own Hindu University as well as by reason of the expected establishment of other Universities. I think that the Government of India in view of the above circumstances should be able to see its way to giving us a much larger recurring grant, as also a substantial non-recurring grant for buildings, etc. I do not know at what figure we can put our expectations; but three lakhs a year would perhaps be not thought too much to suggest, and a moiety of the cost of buildings, etc. You can best advise us how to approach the Government in this matter. The University is of course to be a residential one, and the cost of the construction of the necessary hostel and their maintenance and up-keep have also to be taken into consideration.

14. Turning now to the other question, I think that the new University should have if possible the following faculties, viz.—

1. Oriental.

2. Theological.

3. Arts.

4. Science (Pure and Applied).

5. Law.

The Oriental Faculty, the main object of which will be to foster the study of Sanskrit and its literature, etc., will appeal very largely to the public. My idea is that the studies in that Faculty should be directed by a European Sanskrit scholar of standing and experience, assisted by some Indian Professors who should also be scholars of English. In addition to them we shall require a large staff of Pandits of the old class. We should endeavour to collect famous Pandits in every department of Sanskrit learning who are to be found in various parts of India. Benares is the sacred place of the Hindus to which every pious member of that community aspires to go in the evening of his life. I expect that a good number of eminent Pandits would be attracted to it if suitable honorarium or salary is fixed for their support and maintenance and we should soon collect at *Kashi* the best Pandits of India. Another object of the Oriental Faculty should be to collect and bring together all works now extant in Sanskrit, either in print or preserved in manuscripts. There are yet treasured up many valuable works in Native States and in the families of old Pandits to which the Hindu University can obtain access easily. In this work the Pandits will materially assist. The cultivation of the vernaculars would be another feature of the work of that faculty. I think we shall require about Rs. 6,000 a month to begin work on a suitable scale, and the amount will of course have to be increased as the work develops. A large number of Hindu students from all parts of India still come to Benares for study. They maintain themselves with the help of many charities and chhatras now existing in Benares. If the Hindu University open its doors to them we shall then have a class of students who undertake to study Sanskrit not with the object of seeking employment under the Government but for the sake of study itself. The nobility and gentry of India will continue to help the scholars in the manner in which they have been helped in the past and are now being helped. The Sanskrit College at Benares should be affiliated to this Hindu University and should supplement the work of the University in its own special departments.

15. The faculty of Arts and Science would for the present work on the lines of the faculties in these subjects in the existing Universities. The cost of these departments will depend upon the number of chairs which we can establish and the subjects of study that we propose to take up. There is a great demand for technical education in connection with the Hindu University. That however is a branch of instruction which can swallow up any amount of money. The Maharaja of Jodhpur has given Rs. 21,000 a year for a Professor in some technical subject, and I think it may be possible to inaugurate the study of some special branch of technical education. This will come under the heading Applied science for the present—to be expanded into a Faculty of Technology later on.

The faculty of Law will be practically self supporting. We will have to specialise in Hindu Law and its study from original sources.

16. The Hon'ble Rai Pandit Sunder Lal Bahadur in his letter to me says:—

" In the scheme which I outlined in a note prepared by me last year I indicated my views though necessarily on a limited scale. The cost of running the University apart from its tuitional side was to be met from examination fees such as the existing Universities levy. I do not know whether the Government will be prepared to allow us to hold a Matriculation Examination in various centres and recognised schools as the existing Universities do. I should like very much to know how far the Government will be inclined to accede to the suggestions made by us in our letter to the Hon'ble Sir Harcourt Butler, dated the 25th October 1912, which you submitted to Sir Harcourt Butler on behalf of the Society. If the Government in view of the financial position explained by me above considers that we have made out a sufficient case for asking for legislation in the ensuing cold weather, I will be very glad, as soon as the rains set in, to undertake to draft the constitution of the University and its Statutes and Regulations and to shipshape them during the High Court vacation, for submission to the Government to form the basis of discussion. The fundamental points can be settled by personal discussion wherever necessary."

17. I shall be very glad to come and see you in Simla in the second week of May.

Appendix-13

Demi-official letter No. 117-Edn., dated Simla, the 2nd June 1913.

From—The HON'BLE SIR HARCOURT BUTLER, K.C.S.I., C.I.E.,

To—The HON'BLE MAHARAJA SIR RAMESHWAR SINGH BAHADUR, K.C.I.E., of Darbhanga.

I have to thank you for your letter of the 28th April 1913 in which you explain your exact financial position and suggest for my consideration and advice the steps that might now be taken to bring into existence the Hindu University at an early date.

I regret that I am not yet in a position to indicate the lines on which the constitution of the University should be framed. The matter is still under consideration and reference to the Secretary of State is necessary. Nor am I in a position to make any statement as to finance. I would, however, point out that the figure of 50 lakhs attributed to Mr. Sharp was only a rough estimate of the capitalised value of the recurring expenditure probably required to conduct an University of a thousand students, and did not include capital expenditure. Also the Hindu College was valued at 27 not 14 lakhs. But I note your desire to go ahead with the preparation of a scheme and it will perhaps be of some assistance to you to know the conditions the fulfilment of which the Government of India regard as precedent to the introduction of any scheme. These are :—

    (i) That a suitable site be provided ;

    (ii) That the Central Hindu College be transferred to the University ;

    (iii) That a sum of 50 lakhs must be collected. In this amount may be included the capitalised value of the property mentioned in paragraph 6 of your letter and the perpetual grants mentioned in paragraph 9 of your letter, provided the documentary title is satisfactory in the case of the latter and possession of the property has been made over in the case of the former ;

    indicated to you hereafter; University proceed on lines to be

    (v) That a committee appointed for the purpose report that the Central Hindu College is fit to be developed into a residential and teaching University.

Should progress be as satisfactory as you consider that you have reason to hope, I shall be very glad to meet the Hon'ble Rai Pandit Sundar Lal Bahadur during the High Court vacation.

The Secretary of State, as you are aware, has reserved full discretion in regard to every detail of any scheme that may eventually be laid before him.

Appendix-14

THE HINDU UNIVERSITY SOCIETY

REGISTERED UNDER ACT XXI OF 1860.

No. 4010

4, COUPER ROAD,
ALLAHABAD.

14th July, 1913

My Dear Maharaja Saheb Bahadur,

As desired by you the capitalised value of the permanent annual grants of Bikaner, Kashmer and Jodhpur Darbars have been included in the daily report (copy enclosed) and will also be shown in the Statements to the press in future.

A Statement of our total receipts (including interest) in the Bank and as otherwise disposed of has been prepared as called for by you, and is herewith sent.

Yours Sincerely,

To,

The Hon'ble Maharaja Sir Rameshwar Singh Bahadur, K.C.I.E.
Of Darbhanga.

R A N C H I.

Statement of total receipts (including interest) by the Hindu University Society and how they have been disposed of.

----

1. In current account with Banks (including Maharaja Darbhanga's recent donation of one lakh).   Rs. 128373-10-3

2. Investment in 3½ per cent G. P. Notes of the face value of Rs.2335400/- of which the actual value works out.   " 2254052- 6-6

3. Suspense Account.   " 805- 0-0

4. Advance Account.   " 1985- 0-0

5. With Babu Gokul Chand of Calcutta.   " 101- 2-9

6. In hand (including one Share Certificate of Rs.1000/- and one Fixed Deposit receipt for Rs.2000/-).   " 3335- 1-8½

7. Already Spent.   " 28347- 9-9

Grand Total   Rs.2416999- 5-11½

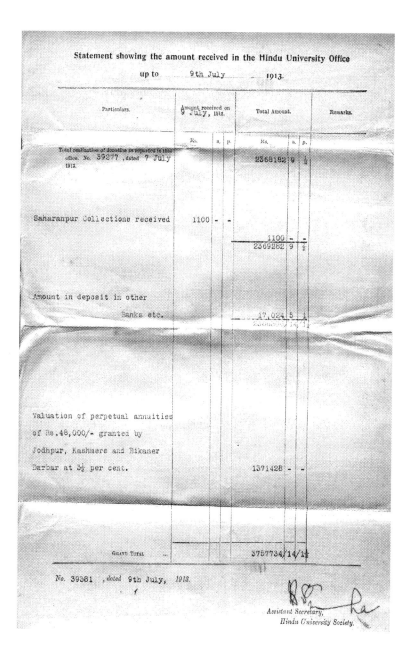

Statement showing the amount received in the Hindu University Office

up to ___9th July___ 1913.

Particulars.	Amount received on 9 July, 1913.			Total Amount.			Remarks.
	Rs.	a.	p.	Rs.	a.	p.	
Total realisation of donation as reported in this office. No. 39277, dated 7 July 1913.				2368182	9	1½	
Saharanpur Collections received	1100	–	–				
				1100	–	–	
				2369282	9	½	
Amount in deposit in other Banks etc.				17,024	5	1	
Valuation of perpetual annuities of Rs.48,000/- granted by Jodhpur, Kashmere and Bikaner Darbar at 3½ per cent.				1371428	–	–	
GRAND TOTAL				3757734	14	1½	

No. 39381 , dated 9th July, 1913.

Assistant Secretary,
Hindu University Society.

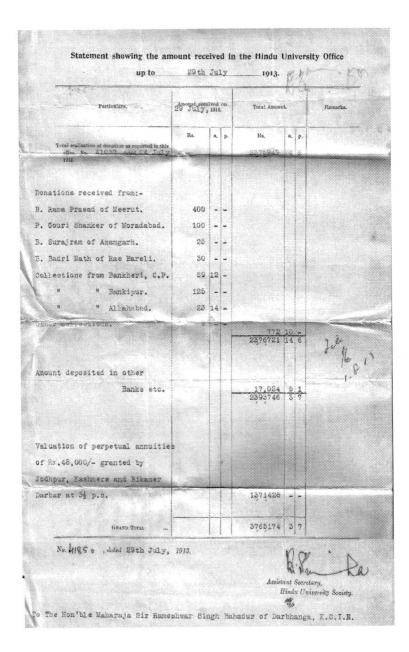

Statement showing the amount received in the Hindu University Office

up to ___29th July___ 1913.

Particulars.	Amount received on 29 July, 1913.			Total Amount.			Remarks.
	Rs.	a.	p.	Rs.	a.	p.	
Total realization of donation as reported in this office. No. 41037 dated 24 July 1913.							
Donations received from:-							
B. Rama Prasad of Meerut.	400	-	-				
P. Gouri Shanker of Moradabad.	100	-	-				
B. Surajram of Azamgarh.	25	-	-				
B. Badri Nath of Rae Bareli.	30	-	-				
Collections from Bankheri, C.P.	59	12	-				
" " Bankipur.	125	-	-				
" " Allahabad.	23	14	-				
Other collections.				772	10	-	
				2376721	14	6	
Amount deposited in other Banks etc.				17,024	5	1	
				2393746	3	7	
Valuation of perpetual annuities of Rs.48,000/- granted by Jodhpur, Kashmere and Bikaner Darbar at 3½ p.c.				1371428	-	-	
GRAND TOTAL ...				3765174	3	7	

No. 41185 , dated 29th July, 1913.

Assistant Secretary,
Hindu University Society.

To The Hon'ble Maharaja Sir Rameshwar Singh Bahadur of Darbhanga, K.C.I.E.

168

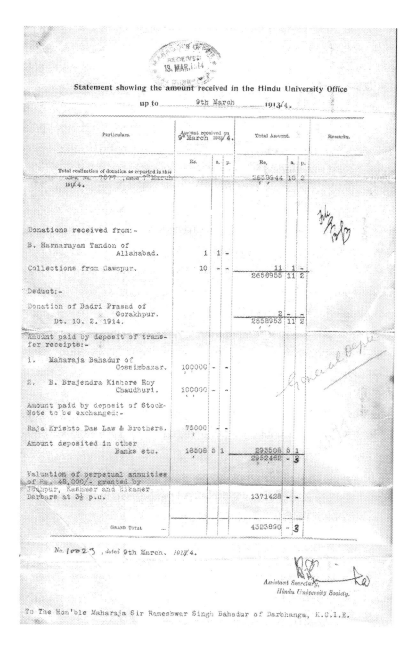

Statement showing the amount received in the Hindu University Office
up to _____ 9th March _____ 1913/4.

Particulars.	Amount received on 9th March 1913/4.			Total Amount.			Remarks.
	Rs.	a.	p.	Rs.	a.	p.	
Total realization of donation as reported in this office, No. 1047, dated 28 February 1913/4.				2658944	10	2	
Donations received from:-							
B. Harnarayan Tandon of Allahabad.	1	1	-				
Collections from Cawnpur.	10	-	-	11	1	-	
				2658955	11	2	
Deduct:-							
Donation of Badri Prasad of Gorakhpur. Dt. 10. 2. 1914.				2	-	-	
				2658953	11	2	
Amount paid by deposit of transfer receipts:-							
1. Maharaja Bahadur of Cossimbazar.	100000	-	-				
2. B. Brajendra Kishore Roy Chaudhuri.	100000	-	-				
Amount paid by deposit of Stock-Note to be exchanged:-							
Raja Krishto Das Law & Brothers.	75000	-	-				
Amount deposited in other Banks etc.	18508	5	1	293508	5	1	
				2952462	-	3	
Valuation of perpetual annuities of Rs. 48,000/- granted by Jaipur, Kashmer and Bikaner Darbars at 3½ p.c.				1371428	-	-	
GRAND TOTAL ...				4323890	-	3	

No. 1023 , dated 9th March. 1913/4.

Assistant Secretary,
Hindu University Society.

To The Hon'ble Maharaja Sir Rameshwar Singh Bahadur of Darbhanga, K.C.I.E.

Statement showing the amount received in the Hindu University Office

up to _____ 4th May _____ 1913/4.

Particulars.	Amount received on 4th May, 1913/4.			Total Amount.			Remarks.
	Rs.	a.	p.	Rs.	a.	p.	
Total realization of donation as reported in this ~~~~ No. ~~~~, dated ~~~~ 1913/4.				2266018	13	2	
Donation received from:-							
B. Harjas Rai of Moradabad.	20	-	-	20	-	-	
				2266108	13	2	
Amount paid by deposit of Transfer Receipts:-							
1. Maharaja Bahadur of Cossimbazar.	100000	-	-				
2. B. Brajendra Kishore Roy Chaudhuri.	100000	-	-				
Amount paid by deposit of Stock Note to be exchanged:-							
Raja Kristo Das Law & Brothers.	75000	-	-				
Amount deposited in other Banks etc.	18508	5	1	293508	5	1	
				3092617	2	3	
Valuation of perpetual annuities of Rs. 48,000/- granted by Jodhpur, Indore and Bikaner ~~~~~~				1371428	-	-	
GRAND TOTAL ...				4464045	2	3	

No. 7636 , dated 4th May. 1913/4.

B. P.
Assistant Secretary,
Hindu University Society.

To The Hon'ble Maharaja Sir Rameshwar Singh Bahadur of Darbhanga, K.C.I.E.

ALWAR.
RAJPUTANA.

31st August 1918.

My dear Maharaja Sahib,

Many thanks for Your Highness' letter
of the 23rd instant.

Regarding the affiliation of our schools
to the Hindu University, I am thinking of talking
this matter over personally with His Excellency
the Viceroy as well as with the Education Member
when I happen to see them at Delhi or Simla.

So far as I can say at present I think
I shall probably be in my capital from December
to February, but it is very difficult to make out
a fixed programme so far ahead.   If Your Highness, however, could give probable dates that
would suit you to visit Alwar, I shall perhaps be
in a position to inform you where I may be likely

to be on those dates.

With kind regards,

Yours sincerely,

ALWAR,
RAJPUTANA.

21st August 1918.

My dear Maharaja Sahib,

Many thanks for Your Highness' letter of the 23rd instant.

Regarding the affiliation of our schools to the Hindu University, I am thinking of talking this matter over personally with His Excellency the Viceroy as well as with the Education Member when I happen to see them at Delhi or Simla.

So far as I can say at present I think I shall probably be in my capital from December to February, but it is very difficult to make out a fixed programme so far ahead. If Your Highness, however, could give probable dates that would suit you to visit Alwar, I shall perhaps be in a position to inform you where I may be likely to be on those dates.

With kind regards,

Yours sincerely,

The Hindu University Society

(Registered under Act XXI of 1860.)

Proceedings of an adjourned meeting of the Committee of Management of the Hindu University Society held at 9, Elgin Road, Allahabad, on the 30th October, at 3 p.m.

PRESENT :

Mahamahopadhyaya Pundit Aditya Ram Bhattacharya, M.A.
The Hon'ble Pundit Madan Mohan Malaviya, B.A., LL.B.
Dr. Satish Chandra Banerji, M.A., LL.D.
The Hon'ble Dr. Tej Bahadur Sapru, M.A., LL.D.
Babu Iswar Saran, B.A.
Babu Bhagwan Das, M.A.
Babu Gauri Shanker Prasad, B.A., LL.B.
Prof. Benoy Kumar Sarkar, M.A.
Pandit Baldev Ram Dave.
The Hon'ble Dr. Sundar Lal, C.I.E., LL.D.

1.   Dr. Satish Chandra Banerji was unanimously voted to the Chair.

2.   In connection with the question of the incorporation of the Central Hindu College, Benares, the resolutions of that body as well as the previous resolutions of the Committee of Management of the Hindu University Society and the letter of Sir Harcourt Butler, dated the 2nd June 1913 were read and considered.

Resolved that the Central Hindu College, Benares, be incorporated with the Hindu University Society subject to the following conditions, *viz* :—

(1)   That all the funds, properties, moveable and immoveable, and all assets held by the said Association as its property, or in trust, and dues belonging to, or owned by it, do vest in, and be transferred to, the Hindu University Society, except the funds expressly endowed for the maintenance of the Central Hindu College Girl's School, as to which the question will be considered at the next meeting of the Committee.

(2)   That the Hindu University Society keep up and maintain the present Central Hindu College with the *Ranavir Pathshala* and the Central Hindu Collegiate School to serve as the nucleus of the Hindu University proposed to be established.

(3)   That for the said purpose the Hindu University Society appoint such Committee or Committees as it may think fit and proper, and define and regulate the powers and the constitution of the said Committee or Committees, and from time to time amend or modify the same.

(4)   That the present trustees of the Central Hindu College be appointed members of the Hindu University Society under Rule 3 (d) of the Rules of this Society, it being always understood that such appointment does not necessitate or require their nomination, or the nomination of any of them, to the membership of the Governing Body of the Hindu University when it is established.

(5)   That the Hindu University Society make such provision as it may think proper from time to time for the maintenance of the said institutions out of the funds which shall vest in it by reason of the

incorporation of the Central Hindu College with it, and to allot at its discretion any further funds it may think proper for the said purpose.

(6) That on the establishment of the Hindu University, the Hindu University Society shall set apart such portion of the funds so transferred to the Hindu University Society from the Central Hindu College as the Hindu University Society may consider proper for the maintenance of the School and shall arrange for its working and governance in such manner as it may consider fit and proper.

3. Resolved that the above Resolution be laid before the Annual General Meeting of the Society to be held on the 2nd December, 1913 and that in the meanwhile it may be communicated to the Secretary, Board of Trustees, Central Hindu College, Benares.

4. Resolved that a Sub-Committee consisting of the Hon'ble Dr. Sundarlal, Dr. Satish Chandra Banerji, the Hon'ble Dr. Tej Bahadur Sapru and Babu Iswar Saran be formed to submit proposals for carrying out the above Resolution and to formulate a Scheme for the proper working of the Central Hindu College, the *Ranavir Pathshala* and the Collegiate School, and that the trustees of the Central Hindu College be requested to nominate three representatives to co-operate with them in preparing the same.

5. Resolved that the above Sub-Committee be also requested to consider and report as to the desirability and feasibility of the Hindu University taking up the management of the Girl's School and its funds and properties. The Sub-Committee to report before the 2nd December, 1913.

6. In connection with Resolution No. 4 of this meeting held on the 26th October, 1913 the Honorary Secretary suggested that the following principle might be adopted in selecting Banks with which arrangements might be made for the receipt and transmission of donations from outstations.

(1) That the Bank or Banks selected should have an office or branch at Allahabad, Benares or Lucknow.

(2) That the Banks should agree to transmit the monies paid in to them or their branches free of charge to Allahabad as promptly as possible.

(3) That notice of payments made by district committees or donors be regularly sent to this Office as soon as practicable after such payment and that the Government Promissory Notes which may be ordered to be purchased through them be purchased and forwarded to this office at a rate not exceeding 0-2-0 per cent.

(4) That the District Committees and donors be requested to deal as far as possible with the Bank of Bengal or its branch if there be one in their district ; and to transmit monies as early as convenient to Allahabad.

The suggestions were approved and adopted and were to be given effect to in revising the list of Banks.

With a vote of thanks to the Chair the meeting dispersed.

SUNDAR LAL,   SATISH CHANDRA BANERJI,
Honorary Secretary.   *Chairman.*

Alwar
Rajputana.

My dear Maharaja Sahib,

Thanks for your kind letter of the 26th ultimo. Perhaps Pdt. Malviaji has communicated to you the result of my conversation with the Viceroy and the Hon'ble Mr. Butler on the subject of the Hindu University. I hope that the matter may be arranged satisfactorily in the end.

With kind regards,

Yours sincerely,

Jey Singh.

P.9.o.

The Hon'ble

Sir Rameshwar Singh K. C. I. E.,
Maharaja Bahadur of
Durbhanga (Behar).

THE HINDU UNIVERSITY SOCIETY

REGISTERED UNDER ACT XXI OF 1860.

No. 1220

To

4, COUPER ROAD,
ALLAHABAD

10 December, 1913.

The Hon'ble Maharaja Sir Rameshwar Singh Bahadur, K.C.I.E

D a r b h a n g a.

My dear Sir,

I am glad to inform you that at the Second Annual General Meeting of this Society held on the 7th instant you were unanimously reelected as President of the Committee of Management of the Society for the ensuing year.

Yours Sincerely,

Honorary Secretary.

Appendix-19

X11/7

Demi-official No. 202-Education.

Simla, the 18th July 1914.

MY DEAR MAHARAJA BAHADUR,

Please refer to my letter to you, No. 117-Education, dated Simla, the 2nd June 1913, in which I regretted that I was not yet in a position to indicate the lines on which the constitution of the University should be framed, as the matter was still under consideration and reference to His Majesty's Secretary of State was necessary, but noted your desire to go ahead with the preparation of a scheme and thought it would be of assistance to you to know the conditions the fulfilment of which the Government of India regarded as necessarily precedent to the introduction of any scheme. These were :—

" (*i*) That a suitable site be provided ;

(*ii*) That the Central Hindu College be transferred to the University ;

(*iii*) That a sum of 50 lakhs must be collected. In this amount may be included the capitalised value of the property mentioned in paragraph 8 of your letter,* and the perpetual grants mentioned in paragraph 9 of your letter, provided the documentary title is satisfactory in the case of the latter and possession of the property has been made over in the case of the former ;

*Dated Darbhanga, 26th April 1913.

(*iv*) That the constitution of the University proceed on lines to be indicated to you hereafter ;

(*v*) That a committee appointed for the purpose report that the Central Hindu College is fit to be developed into a residential and teaching University."

2. I understand that substantial progress· has been made in regard to (*i*), (*ii*) and (*iii*), and action can at any time be taken under (*v*).

As regards (*iv*), I am now in a position to make a further important communication to you.

3. It has been an understanding throughout that in essentials and especially in regard to their relations to Government the proposed Hindu and Muhammadan Universities should be on the same footing. As you are aware, the Muhammadan University Committee have not accepted the constitution laid down in the case of the proposed Muhammadan University at Aligarh. As regards the relations of the proposed University to Government, the original proposal of the Muhammadan University Committee was that the Viceroy should be Chancellor with powers of intervention and control. It was decided, and finally decided, that this should not be. The scheme offered to the

University Committee left the University, through the Court, power to appoint their own Chancellor while it gave the Governor-General in Council the necessary powers of intervention and control. This arrangement was considerably criticised at the time. In consequence the Government of India and His Majesty's Secretary of State have reconsidered the whole question with every desire to assist a solution. They recognise that the Government of India is an impersonal body situated at a distance and cannot give that close personal attention to the University which is required in the case of a new institution of a novel type in India. On a review of all the circumstances of the case, and the criticisms which have been advanced, the Government of India and His Majesty's Secretary of State have come to the conclusion that the best form of constitution will be to constitute the Lieutenant-Governor of the United Provinces *ex-officio* Chancellor of the University with certain opportunities for giving advice and certain powers of intervention and control. The Hindu University, though not empowered to affiliate colleges from outside, will be Imperial in the sense that, subject to regulations, it will admit students from all parts of India. On the other hand, it will be localised in or by Benares. There will be obvious advantages in having as Chancellor of the University the Lieutenant-Governor of the Province, who is also Chancellor of the Allahabad University, and who will be able to help to correlate the work between the two, to secure them corresponding advantages, and to foster a spirit of healthy co-operation. Moreover, such a constitution is in accord with the general policy of decentralization which is now pursued by the Government of India.

4. As regards the powers which it is necessary to reserve to the Chancellor, these are :—

(a) The right of general supervision and power to advise that such action be taken and such staff be appointed or removed as will secure the objects of the University, with power, if necessary, to see that such advice be given effect to.

(b) The right of inspection for purposes of seeing whether the standard of education is kept up sufficiently high and for other purposes.

(c) The right, as a special measure, to appoint, if necessary (as the result of such inspection or otherwise), examiners for the University examinations, who would report to the Chancellor.

(d) The annual receipt of accounts.

(e) The approval of the appointments of Vice-Chancellor and Provost.

(f) The approval of initial regulations, etc., and of subsequent changes.

(g) The approval of the incorporation of local colleges in the University.

(h) The nomination of five members to the Senate ; and

(i) The approval of the institution of new faculties and the reservation of power to lay down the limits of expansion at any particular time.

Some of these powers have been suggested by your Committee. Others are emergency powers which may never be exercised and can be exercised only very occasionally. The principle underlying them all is that in the interest of the rising generation and the parents, the Government must be in co-operation with the University and in a position to help it effectively and secure sound finance. The interests of the Government and the students and their parents in this matter are necessarily identical.

5. As you are already aware, the decision in regard to affiliation of outside colleges is final. It was realised at the time that this decision would cause some disappointment; but I may take this opportunity to observe that it was not reached without due notice to the University Committees. At an informal meeting of the Constitution Committee of the Muhammadan University, held at Simla on the 23rd September 1911, I told the Committee that this question of affiliation might come prominently forward; that there had been a great deal of criticism of the idea of denominational Universities, especially in so far as they cut across existing territorial jurisdictions; that the chief justification of the Aligarh University was that it would be a teaching as opposed to an examining university, that the young men who got their degrees and diplomas of the University would have imbibed the spirit of Aligarh which could not be acquired elsewhere. I again drew attention to the matter at a subsequent meeting held on the 27th of the same month. In an informal discussion with the promoters of the Hindu University, held at the Town Hall, Delhi, on the 4th December 1911, I clearly pointed out the difficulties which beset the proposal to grant affiliation. I mention this because there has been some misunderstanding on the point.

6. In order to meet the sentiment of the subscribers, it has been conceded that the University shall be called the Benares Hindu University. It will have no religious test and will be open to students of all denominations as well as to Hindus. Hindu theological teaching and observances will not be compulsory for any but Hindus. It will also be a teaching and residential University.

7. The terms mentioned above represent the conditions the acceptance of which is necessarily precedent to the elaboration of any detailed scheme. I hope that your Committee will realise that they are worked out in the best interests of the University and the Government, whose close association with it is essential. If they are not all that some of the subscribers may desire, they will enable you to realise an aspiration which a large body of opinion thought impracticable at the outset and which had been rejected by the Universities Commission of 1902. Should your Committee accept the conditions, details of the constitution can be settled. Sir James Meston will be at Allahabad on the 26th instant and will be ready to discuss the matter with us there.

I may add that His Majesty's Secretary of State reserves his final decision on the details of the constitution of the University until they are before him in the form of a draft bill and regulations.

In conclusion I have to state that when a satisfactory scheme has been evolved the Government of India will be glad to show their interest in the new

University by making a liberal financial grant-in-aid. His Majesty's Secretary of State, the Government of India and the Local Government have only one object, *viz.*, to assist your Committee to start this new and interesting experiment on lines best calculated to secure its success, and in so doing to cultivate and promote that enthusiasm for sound education which all who wish well to India whole-heartedly desire.

Yours sincerely,

HARCOURT BUTLER.

The HONB'LE MAHARAJA BAHADUR SIR RAMESHWAR SINGH, K.C.I.E., of Darbhanga.

THE HINDU UNIVERSITY SCHEME.

SIR HARCOURT BUTLER'S LETTER.

THE following is the full text of the letter addressed by the Hon. Sir Harcourt Butler to the Hon. the Maharaja of Durbhanga :—

Simla, 18th July, 1911.—My Dear Maharaja Bahadur,—Please refer to my letter to you, No. 117 Education, dated Simla, the 2nd June, 1913, in which I regretted that I was not yet in a position to indicate the lines on which the constitution of the university should be framed, as the matter was still under consideration, and reference to His Majesty's Secretary of State was necessary, but noted your desire to go ahead with the preparation of a scheme and thought it would be of assistance to you to know the conditions the fulfilments of which the Government of India regarded as necessarily precedent to the introduction of any scheme.

These were :—

(i) That a suitable site be provided.

(ii) That the Central Hindu College be transferred to the university.

(iii) That a sum of Rs. 50 lakhs must be collected. In this amount may be included the capitalised value of the property mentioned in paragraph 6 of your letter and the perpetual grants mentioned in paragraph 9 of your letter provided the documentary title is satisfactory in the case of the latter and possession of the property has been made over in the case of the former.

(iv) That the constitution of the university proceeds on lines to be indicated to you hereafter.

(v) That the committee appointed for the purpose report the Central Hindu College is fit to be developed into a residential and teaching university.

I understand that substantial progress has been made in regard to (i) and (ii) and action can at any time be taken under (v).

As regards (iv), I am now in a position to make further important communication to you.

It has been an understanding throughout that in essentials, and especially in regard to their relations to Government, the proposed Hindu and Mahomedan universities should be on the same footing. As you are aware, the Mahomedan University Committee have not accepted the constitution laid down in the case of the proposed University by Government. The original proposal of the Mahomedan University Committee was that the Viceroy should be Chancellor with powers of intervention and control. It was decided—and finally decided—that this should not be. The scheme offered to the University Committee left the University through the court power to appoint their own Chancellor, while it gave the Governor-General in Council the necessary power of intervention and control. This arrangement was considerably criticised at the time. In consequence the Government of India and His Majesty's Secretary of State have reconsidered the whole question with every desire to assist a solution. They recognise that the Government of India is an impersonal body, situated at a distance, and cannot give that close personal attention to the university which is required in the case of a new institution of a novel type in India. On a review of all the circumstances of the case and the criticisms which have been advanced, the Government of India and His Majesty's Secretary of State have come to the conclusion that the best form of constitution will be to constitute the Lieutenant-Governor of the United Provinces *ex officio* Chancellor of the University, with certain opportunities for giving advice and certain powers of intervention and control. The Hindu University, though not empowered to affiliate colleges from outside, will be Imperial in the sense that, subject to regulations, it will admit students from all parts of India. On the other hand, it will be localised in or by Benares. There will be obvious advantages in having as Chancellor of the University the Lieutenant-Governor of the Province, who is also Chancellor of the Allahabad University and who will be able to help to correlate the work between the two, to secure them corresponding advantages and to foster a spirit of healthy co-operation. Moreover, such a constitution is in accord with the general policy of decentralisation which is now pursued by the Government of India.

As regards the powers which it is necessary to reserve to the Chancellor these are :—

(*a*). The right of general supervision and power to advise that such action be taken and such staff be appointed or removed as will secure the objects of the university, with power if necessary to see that such advice be given effect to.

(*b*). The right of inspection for purposes of seeing whether the standard of education is kept up sufficiently high and for other purposes.

(c) The right, as a special measure, to appoint if necessary (as the result of such inspection or otherwise) examiners for the University Examinations who would report to the Chancellor.

(d) The annual receipt of accounts.

(e) The approval of the appointments of Vice-Chancellor and Provost.

(f) The approval of initial regulations, etc., and of subsequent changes.

(g) The approval of the incorporation of local Colleges in the University.

(h) The nomination of five members to the Senate and

(i) Approval of the institution of new faculties and the reservation of power to lay down the limits of expansion at any particular time.

Some of these powers have been suggested by your committee, others are emergency powers which may never be exercised and can be exercised only very occasionally. The principle underlying them all is that in the interest of the rising generation and the parents the Government must be in co-operation with the University and in a position to help it effectively and secure sound finance. The interest of the Government and the students and their parents in this matter are necessarily identical.

As you are already aware, the decision in regard to affiliation of outside colleges is final. It was realised at the time that this decision would cause some disappointment ; but I may take this opportunity to observe that it was not reached without due notice to the University Committee. At an informal meeting of the Constitution Committee of the Mahomedan University, held at Simla on the 23rd September, 1911, I told the Committee that this question of affiliation might come prominently forward, that there had been a great deal of criticism of the idea of denominational universities, especially in so far as they cut across existing territorial jurisdiction ; that the chief justification of the Aligarh University was that it would be a teaching as opposed to an examining university : that the young men who got their degrees and diplomas of the university would have imbibed the spirit of Aligarh which could not be acquired elsewhere. I again drew attention to the matter at a subsequent meeting on the 27th of the same month in an informal discussion with the promoters of the Hindu University held in the Town Hall, Delhi, on the 4th December, 1911. I clearly pointed out the difficulties which beset the proposal to grant affiliation. I mentioned this because there has been some misunderstanding on the point.

In order to meet the sentiment of the subscribers it has been conceded that the university shall be called the Benares Hindu University. It will have no religious test and will be open to students of all denomination as well as to Hindus, Hindu theological teaching and observances will not be compulsory for any but Hindus. It will also be a teaching and residential university.

The terms mentioned above represent the conditions the acceptance of which is necessarily precedent to the elaboration of any detailed scheme. I hope that your committee will realise that they are worked out in the best interests of the university and the Government whose close association with it is essential. If they are not all that some of the subscribers may desire they will enable you to realise an aspiration which a large body of opinion thought impracticable at the outset and which had been rejected by the Universities Commission of 1902. Should the committee accept the conditions, details of the constitution can be settled. Sir James Meston will be at Allahabad on the 26th instant and will be ready to discuss the matter with us there. I may add that His Majesty's Secretary of State reserves his final decision on the details of the constitution of the university until they are before him in the form of a draft bill and regulations. In conclusion, I have to state that when a satisfactory scheme has been envolved the Government of India will be glad to show their interest in the new university by making a liberal financial grant in-aid. His Majesty's Secretary of State, the Government of India and the Local Government have only one object, viz., to assist your committee to start this new and interesting experiment on the lines best calculated to secure its success and in so doing to cultivate and promote that enthusiasm for sound education, which all who wish well to India wholeheartedly desire.—Yours sincerely, HARCOURT BUTLER.

Private & Confidential.

Simla.

19.July 1914.

My dear Maharaja Bahadur,

Herewith the letter in original with one hundred printed copies.

May I congratulate you on having carried the movement so far. I hope your people will be reasonable and that we shall soon work out a good scheme.

With all good wishes

Yours very sincerely,

Sd.Harcourt Butler.

XII/7

Viceregal Lodge,

Simla.

The 22nd July 1914.

My dear Maharaja,

I know H.E. was deeply touched by the real
and true sympathy that you have shown him in his
great sorrow.

I asked him about that foundation stone
and he says he has no objection to your telling
your Hindu friends & the Chiefs when you contemplate
visiting that the Viceroy takes a very great interest
in the movement and if all goes well you may look
forward to his laying the foundation stone of the
University in the winter. I hope this will as you
say make your path easier and give more power to
your elbow.

Believe me,

Yours very sincerely,

Sd.J.H.DuBoulay.

Private Secretary.

Nawab House, Jaipur.
The 26th July 1914.

My dear Maharaja Sahib,

I write to acknowledge with many thanks the receipt of Your Highness three letters dated the 16th, 20th & 24th instants. I am really very happy to find that the establishment of the Hindu University has at last been sanctioned by the Secretary of State and I congratulate Your Highness on the success of your noble efforts.

I sincerely wish that the time may soon arrive when the Mohammadan University will also come into existence, so that both the sister Universities may prosper side by side and improve the condition of the two communities and with the dawn of the light of education they may open a new era in the annals of two great communities in India.

It is needless for me to say that it would give me the greatest pleasure to receive Your Highness here on a mission like this. But I regret very much to say that, of late, His Highness has not been keeping in good health - And moreover he is very much disturbed in mind owing to the illness of Lalji Sahib, Genga Singh.

The boy is motherless and is a great favourite of His Highness. I therefore think that your visit at such a time would neither be opportune nor it will have the desired result. Hoping this will find you in the enjoyment of good health. With my kindest regards,

Believe me

Yours sincerely,

Sd.Md.Faiyaz Alikhan.

Appendix-23

Demi-official letter from the Hon'ble Maharaja Bahadur Sir Rameshwar Singh, K.C.I.E., of Darbhanga, to the Hon'ble Sir Harcourt Butler, K.C.S.I., C.I.E., I.C.S., dated the 21st August 1914.

As I informed you at Allahabad there is considerable apprehension regarding the terms and conditions laid down in your letter to me no. 22, dated the 18th July 1914. I think that if you would authorise me to place before the meeting of the 31st instant, informally, the substance of our conversation at Allahabad with Sir James Meston, Pundit Sunder Lal and Pundit Madan Mohan Malaviya, much of that apprehension would be removed, and the intentions of the Government of India would be more clearly appreciated. I refer particularly to paragraph 4 of your letter with special reference to the appointment of professors, the scope of inspection, the method of appointing examiners, the approval of the incorporation of local colleges in the University, the approval of the institution of new faculties and the reservation of power to lay down the limits of expansion at any particular time. I feel certain that the supporters of the movement would be genuinely grateful for a further pronouncement on these points before the meeting takes place.

Demi-official letter from the Hon'ble Sir Harcourt Butler, K.C.S.I., C.I.E., I.C.S., to the Hon'ble Maharaja Bahadur Sir Rameshwar Singh, K.C.I.E., of Darbhanga, no. 810, dated the 22nd August 1914.

I am obliged to you for your letter of yesterday's date. I have no objection to your placing informally before the meeting of your Committee of the 31st August the substance of our conversation at Government House, Allahabad, under the Presidency of Sir James Meston. There has undoubtedly been misconception in certain quarters regarding paragraph 4 of my letter to you, which appears to be readily susceptible of removal.

2. In the first place I would point out that the words used in paragraph 4 of my letter were not intended to give more than the substance of the terms and conditions required. Verbal precision and definition must be left until the necessary enactment is drafted in the Legislative Department of the Government of India. I now deal with the terms of paragraph 4 of my letter *seriatim.*

3. The appointment of professors will be in the hands of the University. This was settled in the case of the proposed University at Aligarh and the Government of India have no intention of altering the procedure in the case of the Benares Hindu University. The words " and such staff be appointed " referred merely to the power of the Chancellor to secure that the scale of staff was sufficiently strong for the objects of the University. I may point out that the necessity for such a provision is recognised in clause 9 (3) of the draft Hindu University Bill which was handed to me by the Honorary Secretary of your Committee on 23rd October 1912. I may add that the power of removal is explicitly given in the same clause.

4. The right of inspection or visitation is provided for in clauses 9 (1) and 12 of the draft Bill. The object of this condition is to secure that the standard of education is kept sufficiently high and that the University is run on lines generally approved.

5. Paragraph 4 (c) of my letter contemplated leaving examinations in ordinary times entirely in the hands of the University authorities but reserved an emergency power to appoint examiners in the event of the standards of examination deteriorating. Clause 28 of the draft Bill provides as a regular procedure that at least one external and independent examiner shall be appointed for each subject or group of subjects. Should your Committee prefer such a rule with the condition that the appointment of the external and internal examiners would be subject to the approval of the Chancellor, the Government of India, with the concurrence of Sir James Meston, will recommend this modification of the terms to the Secretary of State.

6. The annual receipt of accounts—(d) of my letter ; the approval of initial regulations—(f) of my letter ; and the nomination of five members of the Senate—(h) of my letter ; are directly or indirectly covered by the provisions of clauses 16, 32 and 9 (2) of the draft Bill.

7. Clause 10 of the draft Bill provided that the appointment of Vice-Chancellor should be subject to the approval of the Governor-General in Council.

8. The approval of the incorporation of local colleges in a teaching and residential University—(g) of my letter—is analogous to the affiliation of a college to an affiliating University. In the case of the latter the sanction of Government is required under section 21 of the Indian Universities Act, 1914.

Clause 19 of the draft Bill requires the sanction of the Governor-General in Council for the institution of new faculties. There is no intention to fetter the ordinary development of the University but new additions to the University would naturally require the approval of the Chancellor, who will necessarily be deeply interested in the growth and prosperity of the University.

I need scarcely add that in taking powers to intervene where necessary in the affairs of the University, the Government of India and the Local Government are animated by a desire to help a new experiment rather than to coerce it. It is far from their intention to crush initiative and enterprise on the part of the University authorities as some critics of the scheme appear to imagine.

2   The Hindoo Patriot, January 11, 1913

The Hindu University.

THE correspondence between Sir Harcourt Butler and the Maharaja Bahadur of Durbhanga, which has recently been published, has been read with unmixed satisfaction by educated Hindus all over India. It holds out a reasonably certain prospect of the Hindu University scheme being materialised at no distant day. Verily, Sir Harcourt Butler could not have more appropriately signalised his relinquishment of the portfolio of Education than by setting the seal of the approval of the Government upon a scheme the success of which has been the foremost in the thoughts of the Hindu community for the past few years. In the Maharaja Bahadur of Durbhanga, the promoters have found a superb leader whose enthusiasm is equalled only by his sobriety and the future historian of the Hindu University will delight to dwell upon those highly successful tours of the Maharaja Bahadur from one end of the country to the other, which had brought such substantial accessions to its funds in all the successive stages of the movement. In his letter dated the 14th November last, the Maharaja Bahadur of Durbhanga wrote demi-officially to Sir Harcourt Butler expressing the gratitude of the Hindu University Society for a favourable decision as to the name and for the "very great interest" taken by the Government and for their liberal offer of grant-in-aid. The Society was however disappointed that its proposal that the Viceroy should be the Chancellor of the University should have been vetoed by the Secretary of State. Having regard however to the All-India character of the proposed Hindu University, the Maharaja Bahadur went on to submit that it would not be quite in keeping with the dignity of the University to have the Lieutenant Governor as Chancellor, though the Society reposed the fullest confidence in Sir James Meston. Accordingly, the Maharaja Bahadur ventured to suggest, as an alternative proposal, that the Lieutenant Governor should be a Visitor, as in modern English Universities, that the University should be allowed to elect its own Chancellor and that the powers proposed to be vested in the Viceroy should be exercised by the Government of India.

In his demi-official reply, dated the 23rd December last, Sir Harcourt Butler, speaking for the Government of India, wrote that he was very glad indeed to be able to assure the Maharaja Bahadur that "there is now a bright prospect for a successful issue of our labours and discussion." He pointed out that nothing could be farther from the truth than to insinuate, as had been done in certain quarters, that the conditions imposed by the Government of India would "deprive the University of freedom and hamper its development." So far from this being the case, the Hindu University would in certain respects enjoy "more freedom than other Universities in India." For instance, to quote Sir Harcourt Butler's language, "it has been decided, to allow the University to elect its own Chancellor and Vice-Chancellor, to appoint its own Professors, Lecturers and Staff, to appoint its own examiners, and to conduct its own internal administration. Certain appointments will require approval and certain powers are reserved to the Government, but I anticipate that the work of the University will be conducted by the University itself exercising a larger measure of independence. It is very far from the wish of Sir James Meston, the Government of India and His Majesty's Secretary of State to deprive the University of the privileges which are necessary for its dignity and usefulness." Under the arrangements proposed, Sir Harcourt Butler went on to point out, the Viceroy will be a Patron, while the Lieutenant Governor will be an ex-officio Visitor, vested with powers corresponding to those which the Government or Chancellor now ordinarily exercises in the case of existing Universities. The emergency powers, which are of a purely precautionary character and sure to be most sparingly exercised, will rest with the Government of India.

[Photo]   [R. K. Mullen.]
Babu Saranba Chandra Mallro.
President, Theistic Conference, held at Madras in December, 1912.

We venture to think that this is an eminently satisfactory settlement and ought to be acceptable even to the most exacting. Governments and Governors have other things to occupy themselves with than to be perpetually finding fault with the working of a University of the unique character of the proposed Hindu University. The Government here added met the University Committee more than half way and after all ours is a world of compromises and compromises. We are indebted for these valuable concessions as much to the generosity of our enlightened Government as to the tact and sagacity of the Maharaja Bahadur of Durbhanga and the moderation and fairness of Pundit Madan Mohan, Dr. Sunderlal and other prominent protagonists of the Hindu University movement. The draft Bill submitted by the University Society will have to be redrafted, for, to again quote Sir Harcourt's language, "we should have to be guided eventually" so far as mere drafting goes, "by the expert advice of the Legislative Department of the Government of India." Then the amended Bill and initial regulation will have to be again submitted to the Secretary of State for his final sanction but Sir Harcourt does not anticipate any further difficulties and henceforth it will be all plain sailing.

In conclusion, we must congratulate Sir Harcourt Butler on the successful issue of this great scheme. His lengthy dissertations on different aspects of the educational problem, which he delighted in publishing, from time to time in the guise of Departmental Resolutions, laying down the programme for the next fifty years or so, may be forgotten. But his name will go down to posterity as that of the Education Minister during whose tenure of office the Hindu University scheme practically became all but an accomplished fact.

SIR H. BUTLER'S SPEECH.

Sir Harcourt Butler, in introducing the Hindu University Bill said :—My Lord, I move to introduce the Benares Hindu University Bill. It is the earnest desire of the University committee that this measure may be placed upon the Statute Book during the Viceroyalty of Your Excellency, with whose name the University will be for ever associated. It is but bare truth that without your Excellency's constant interest, support and approval, this measure could not have been introduced to-day. By a series of compromises the Government and the Society have arrived at conclusions which, I hope, may take the measure out of the domain of controversy. It is intended to publish the Bill now for general information and to take the select committee stage and pass the Bill into law during the September session. Before I go further I must congratulate the committee, and especially the Maharaja Bahadur of Durbhanga, Mrs. Besant, Dr. Dunder Lall, Pandit Madan Mohan Malaviya, Rai Bahadur Ganga Prosad Varma, Sir Gooroo Dass Bannerji, Dr. Rash Behari Ghose, and outside the committee such active helpers as the Maharaja of Bikanir and the Maharaja of Benares, on the success which has already crowned their efforts. I need not review the history of the movements which resulted in proposals for the Hindu University at Benares and the Moslem University at Alligarh. I will deal with the results that have emerged from long discussions. The facts are well known, but I will confidently say this, that if anyone had predicted ten years ago, that the idea of a university of this kind then in the air would take practical shape he simply would not have been believed. The University Commission, an influential body, had recently pronounced against such a university and there was a widespread opposition and hostility to any scheme which threatened to cut into the existing territorial and federal

...day. At the same time, there is naturally a very little knowledge in the country of what a teaching and a residential university is. To this want of knowledge I attribute much of the criticism which has been levelled against the constitution of the Benares Hindu University.

The conditions which are appropriate and necessary in a teaching and residential university have been viewed awry through the glasses of minds habituated to existing universities. This is only natural in the circumstances of India. I wish it were possible to say in a few words what a teaching and residential university really means. Probably the best idea will be obtained from Cardinal Newman's idea of a university. May I quote a passage from the report of the Commission on University Education in London, the most authoritative statement of modern times on university education? It runs as follows: In the first place it is essential that regular students of a university should be able to work in intimate and constant association with their fellow students, not only of the same but of different faculties, and also in close contact with their teachers. The university should be organised on this basis and should regard it as the ordinary and normal state of things. This is impossible, however, when any considerable proportion of students are not fitted by previous training to receive university education and therefore do not and cannot take their place in the common life of the university as a community of teachers and students, but as far as their intellectual education is concerned continue in a state of pupilage and receive instruction of much the same kind as at school though under conditions of greater individual freedom. It is good that students should be brought together, if only in this way, and Cardinal Newman, writing in 1852 even went so far as to say: I protest to you, gentlemen, that if I had to choose between a so called university which dispensed with residence and tutorial superintendence, and gave its degrees to any person who passed an examination in a wide range of subjects, and a university which had no professors or examinations at all but merely brought a number of young men together for three or four years and then sent them away, as the university of Oxford is said to have done some sixty years since, if we asked which of these two methods was better for the discipline of intellect which of the two courses was more successful in the training, moulding and enlarging of the mind, which sent out men more fitted for their secular duties, which produced better public men, men of the world, men whose names would descend to posterity, I have no hesitation in giving the preference to that university which did nothing over that which exacted of its members and acquaintance with every science under the sun."

CO-OPERATION OF TEACHERS AND STUDENTS.

Nevertheless this is only one side of the question and in any case Cardinal Newman does not refer to the kind of student life that can be reproduced in London. But, for this very reason, it is more essential that in such a university as London can have students and teachers should be brought together in living intercourse in the daily work of the university. From the time the undergraduate enters the university he should find himself a member of the community in which he has his part to play. Teaching and learning should be combined through the active and personal co-operation of teachers and students. The Association on more or less fraternal lines is the keynote of a teaching and a residential university and it does not aim at mere intellectual attainment overhung by examinations. It is the way of life and the way of corporate life. Those of us who have been at Oxford or Cambridge can appreciate the force and meaning of Cardinal Newman's vivid words. But Oxford and Cambridge are not the only models. There is much to be learned in India from other universities which are more definitely practical in aim. They are all, however, alike in this, that their outlook on life forms an atmosphere of concentrated thought and by friction of minds get truer perspectives, no matter whether the dominant note be philosophic or technic.

So much for the teaching and residential aspect of the university. There remains the question of religious instruction. You know the history of religious instruction in India, the fixed count of the organisation of the new university. You will see that it is a somewhat complicated organisation and it has been necessary to define and adjust the functions with some care. The university is an All-India university. It is incorporated for the teaching of all knowledge but will commence with five faculties—arts, science, law, oriental studies, and theology. I know that many of the promoters desire to add the faculty of technology. This desire has my full sympathy and I trust that adequate funds will soon be forthcoming. The university will be open to students from all parts of India on conditions which I shall specify hereafter. The Governor-General is Lord Rector and the Lieut.-Governor of the United Provinces of Agra and Oudh is the visitor of the University. Among those whom the university will delight to honour are patrons, vice-patrons and rectors. The governing body is numerous and very representative; the court with an executive body in council of not more than 30 members, of whom five will be members of the senate. The academic body is the senate, consisting of not less than 50 members, with an executive body in the syndicate. The senate will have entire charge of the organisation of instruction in the university and its constituent colleges, the curriculum and examination, the discipline of students and the conferment of ordinary and honorary degrees. Except in matters reserved to it the senate is under the control of the court, working through the Council. The senate will be constituted as follows:— ex-officio (a) Chancellor, pro-Chancellor, vice-Chancellor and the pro-vice-Chancellor for the time being; (b) university professors; (c) principals or heads of constituent colleges of the university, 11 Elected (a) five members to be elected by the court; (b) five members to be elected by the registered graduates of the University from such date as the court may fix; (c) five representatives of the Hindu religion, and Sanskrit learning, to be elected by the Senate; (d) Should the vice-Chancellor declare that there is a deficiency in the number of members required in any faculty or faculties then five or less persons elected by the Senate, eminent in the subject or subjects of that faculty or those faculties; three nominated and five members to be nominated by the visitor. The syndicate will consist of a vice-Chancellor, pro-vice-Chancellor and fifteen members of whom not less than ten shall be University professors, or principals or professors of constituent colleges. The object aimed at is to secure that purely academic matters should be decided by a body mainly expert, while the government and supervision of the University rests with the Court and Council. It is necessary to represent the Senate on the latter in order that the academic view may always be before it. The Court will elect its own Chancellor and pro-Chancellor, vice-Chancellor and pro-vice-Chancellor. In the first instance these officers will be scheduled. The Vice-Chancellor will be ex-official chairman of the Council, Senate and Syndicate. He will be the chief executive officer of the university. The university will, through the council and board of appointments, appoint its own professors and staff and have entire control over them. Stability is given to its constitution by requiring the sanction of an external authority to changes in statutes and regulations. This is the outline of the constitution of the university.

SOME CRITICISMS MET.

The Government binds itself to accept degrees, etc., of this university as equivalent to degrees, etc., of existing universities. This in itself is no mean concession. My Lord, I have seen this constitution described as illiberal and I have rubbed my eyes in amazement. It is far more liberal than the constitution of the existing universities. No Government can allow universities to grow up without control. In most European countries universities, or at least the majority of them, are entirely State universities. In the course of these discussions two policies emerged. One was the policy of trust and the other a policy of distrust. The Government might well have said to society "You are starting a new kind of university without any experience in India. We must leaven it with officials who have the requisite experience. We must guide you from within, at any rate until you prove your worth and the value of your degrees." That would not have been an unreasonable attitude. But we preferred to trust society, to leave them large autonomy, and to reserve to subject to the approval of the Chancellor. In the case of this University only 5 out of a minimum of 50 are nominated by the visitor who is ex-officio the Lieutenant-Governor of the United Provinces, and this provision was suggested by yourselves in order to secure expert official help and co-operation. In Calcutta the appointment of professors requires the sanction of the Government of India. In this university no such sanction is required. There will be in this university under normal conditions no interference whatever from outside with the university staff. In Calcutta the vice-Chancellor is appointed by the Governor-General in Council. In this university the Court elects the vice-Chancellor, subject only to approval by the visitor. The Court has power to elect its Chancellor and pro-Chancellor. In the Court and Council the Government has no voice or representation whatever. Ordinary powers of intervention are vested in the visitor. The visitor will be close at hand. You will need his help at every turn in the acquisition of land and in many other ways. And you will not appeal to Sir James Meston in vain. Extraordinary powers are vested in the Governor-General in Council. You need not be alarmed lest they be exercised unduly. The tendency will be other way. It will not be in human nature that the visitor should seek lightly the intervention of the Governor-General in Council. I have not noticed such a tendency in local Governments. In the Government of India the tendency is all the other way, to avoid interference in details of administration. The terms are necessarily general but it is made quite clear that they are extraordinary and emergent powers, and, considering how much this movement already owes to the Government of India, I confidently ask you to believe in our *bona fides.*

We have trusted the promoters so much that I think we ourselves may claim some trust at your hands.

ADMISSION TO THE UNIVERSITY.

So much for the constitution of the university. There remains the question of admission to the university and this raises the whole question of recognition of schools and matriculation. This will be dealt with in the regulations but I will tell you exactly what is our policy in this matter and what principles underlie it. Some of the promoters, I understand, desire to keep the recognition of schools in the hands of the University and to conduct their own Matriculation Examination. This wish is opposed to all the best modern view on the subject. The view strongly emphasised by the commission on University education in London that it is the central educational authority which is concerned to see that its grants are effectively used and that it is this authority also, which must provide for the co-ordination of secondary schools and universities and must give necessary assurance to the latter that pupils seeking admission to their degree courses have reached the required standard of education. The Committee, I may mention, accept the recognition of schools by the local Governments and Durbars. As regards matriculation I must remind the Council that this is not a federal territorial university but a teaching and residential university. In the case of Dacca University the committee decided that it would not conduct its own matriculation examination. It was recognised that most of the high school students would be reading for admission to colleges of Calcutta University and that therefore the requirements of that university must regulate the course of studies. In those schools, in the case of the Benares Hindu University, pupils of the high schools will similarly be reading for admission to the visiting universities and the new university could not with advantage set up a different standard or prescribe a new course. Again it was recognised that a separate entrance examination for Dacca, held at the headquarters of Dacca, would be cumbrous and difficult to carry out, and would be likely to cause confusion. These reasons are applicable with even greater force to Benares Hindu University. Probably before many years have passed the external matriculation examination octopus, which digs its tentacles into all the limbs and parts of our secondary English schools, will be replaced by some system of school-leaving certificate. The most weighty authorities of modern times, the Consulative Committee on examinations in secondary schools, and Lord Haldane's Commission on University Education in London, alike contemplate the abolition of purely external matriculation examinato the sentiment or... it will come under reconsideration if at any time the school leaving certificate generally ousts the matriculation examination of other universities.

THE SUBSCRIBERS.

I have now dealt fully and frankly with the two main points on which there have been differences of opinion. There remains yet another point on which there has been a misunderstanding that is easily removable. It is said that this University has ceased to be an All-India University. This is not the case. It is open to students from every province and Native State in India. The school which is preparing for admission to it may be situated in any province or Native State in India. Its governing body is recruited from the length and breadth of India. It will send forth its *alumni* to every quarter of India. It will number among its patron Governors and heads of provinces, Ruling Chiefs and other eminent benefactors in all parts of India. I am informed that the following large subscriptions have already been paid: Maharana of Udaipur 1½ lakhs, Maharaja Holkar 5 lakhs, Maharaja of Jodhpur 2 lakhs, with a grant in perpetuity of Rs. 2,000 a month, Maharaja of Bikanir one lakh with a grant in perpetuity of Rs. 1,000 a month, Maharaja of Kashmir a grant in perpetuity of Rs. 1,000 a month, Maharao of Kota one lakh, Maharaja Bahadur of Darbhanga 3 out of 5 lakhs, Dr. Ras Behari Ghose 1 lakh, Dr. Sunder Lal 1 lakh, Maharaja of Cossimbazar 1 lakh, Babu Brojendra Kishore Roy Chaudhuri of Goureepur 1 lakh, and Babu Moti Chand 1 lakh. The Maharaja Scindia of Gwalior has promised five lakhs of rupees and others have promised liberal donations of which, in many cases, part payment has been made. If there ever was an All-India University it is this. I think that on review of all the facts hon. members will agree that the Government has dealt in a large and liberal spirit with the movement. The conduct of negotiations has n...

easy. It has been complicated by the fact that the movement started on lines of its own without reference to Government and without knowledge of the conditions which Government considered essential to its success. It was further complicated by criticisms from opposing points of view. If to some it has seemed that Government was granting too little, to others it has seemed that Government was granting too much. I do not conceal from Hon. members that in some quarters it has been considered that the Government was taking grave risks—risks graver than any Government ought to face. I can understand this view but I do not myself share it. We know that we are taking a certain amount of risk. We know that there is danger lest this University or similar universities elsewhere develop undesirable tendencies or lower standards of education. We deliberately face that risk, believing in the loyalty and good sense of India, and the growing desire to co-operate with Government on the part of the Hindu and other communities in India. For my part I am hopeful of success. I earnestly trust that the introduction of this Bill and removal of misunderstanding will lead to further enthusiasm and the provision of funds sufficient to build and equip the university on a worthy scale—a scale worthy of the great Hindu community. I confess that the other day, when I stood opposite Ramnagar, on the site where your University buildings will I hope, soon be rising in stately array, and looked down the river Ganges to the ghats at Kashi, which swept before me in the distance, I felt that if I was a Hindu I should be proud indeed of the achievement of my people, and at the same time I felt some little pride myself that I was a member of a Government which had joined in one more large endeavour to combine the ancient and honoured culture of India with the culture of the modern Western world.

Printed in the United States
By Bookmasters